God, I ain't trying to hear all that!

By: Ken Canion

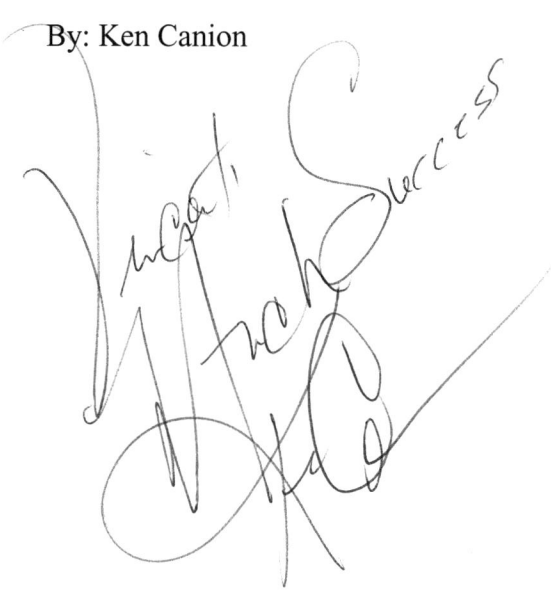

God, I ain't trying to hear all that!

By: Ken Canion

Published by:

Prosperity Marketing
510 Franklin Blvd.
Greensboro, NC 27401

Editing: QS Group, Inc.
Cover Design: Jerome Thompson

Printed in the United States of America

December 2002

ISBN: 0-9676942-1-3

DEDICATION

This book is dedicated to my beautiful wife who supports, encourages and challenges me to follow and fulfill my dreams. It is also dedicated to a father who has shown me how to be strong in tough times and to a mother who has shown me what Godly love truly is.

God, I ain't trying to hear all that!

God, I ain't trying to hear all that!

Everything Happening,
Great and Small,
Is a parable whereby
GOD speaks to us, and the Art of Life
Is to get The Message

Malcom Muggeridge (1903 – 1990)
English journalist and writer

God, I ain't trying to hear all that!

God, I ain't trying to hear all that!

TABLE OF CONTENTS:

God, I ain't trying to hear all that!

INTRODUCTION

What is success? I guess this is as good a place to start as any. Why, you might ask? Well, the answer is simple: because I have been consumed with that very question for most of my life.

For many years I have been seeking the magical formula that would get me to the place I call success. Authors, motivators, preachers, and teachers have all given their take on what and how to achieve it. Books, articles, essays, and speeches have produced valid explanations. I don't plan to add any new revelations about this American obsession, but I do hope to shed new light on the concept of how one might find the answer to their own question of how to find it.

First of all, let us discuss the definition of success. It can mean many things to many people. Each of us must learn and discover what it means to us. Is it money that makes a person successful? Is it position or status? Is it the material possessions they own or the relations they have? Is it a career? Is it because they are in good health? What I've learned over the years has changed my perspective on life, happiness, and especially success. It starts with knowing your strengths and building on them and knowing your weaknesses and working on them.

Not very long ago the only thing I measured success by was financial wealth. If you had money, I thought, you had it going on. My sole objective in life was to make a million dollars. Once I got to that status, everything else would be gravy. I became consumed in reaching this goal in my business life. To me everything else was secondary, and everybody who wasn't helping me get there became secondary as well. The money began rolling in and I started seeing my goal within reach.

Then something happened along the way. All hell broke loose. Everything that could have gone wrong did. The goal that I held so closely seemed to loose its value when I weighed the cost of achieving it. The more I focused on the money the further it seemed to move out of reach. My definition of success began to change. As I went through adversity, God began to change my heart and ultimately my perspective on what success is.

One day my pastor was doing a seminar on success and giving principles that have helped him achieve a measure of success in his life. I was going through a period of self-evaluation and searching for a new outlook. I knew success had to be more than money. I had heard many define it but nothing that really stuck until I heard it that day from Pastor Otis Lockett Sr. He gave a comprehensive definition that captured the essence of what true success was all about. It was from a biblical perspective and he stressed he wasn't talking about money. He was talking about life. Although, he had acquired a measurable level of financial wealth, his definition of success didn't involve money. For me, this was a whole new way of looking at it because my sole definition of success was based on money.

He started by saying: "Success is never ending," and "Failure is not final."

I had heard my grandmother and mother talk about knowing GOD and living for him, but I believed all along that it was just their thing. Sure, I respected what they tried to impart, but it just wasn't for me.

All I could think about was money. My thought process was that if I were a Christian, money and prosperity would be mine for the taking. Again, just keeping it real, I was in it for the money and blessings. I wouldn't learn until later that there was much more to knowing than merely funding my business ventures.

Seek ye first the kingdom of GOD and his righteousness and all these things will be added unto you. (Matthew 6:33)

Growing up I can remember envying people who had talents I wished I had. I was jealous of guys who could run fast, or students who were smarter in math than I was. Even when I got older I envied guys in football or in business who I thought possessed gifts that I didn't. Deep down inside I was overwhelmed with jealously.

Everything we do in life should in some way benefit others. This was the way my mother saw it.

"Yeah, okay, I hear you," I would answer, but in my heart I figured I had to get mine. All that really mattered was getting what belonged to me. Let other people fend for themselves. I guess that is why it always bothered me that my mother would take her hard earned money every week and go feed the men at the homeless shelter. I would say, "These are grown men. Why can't they go get a job and feed themselves? They are a lot healthier than you."

She would look at me with knowing eyes. "Everything we do in life should benefit others. You just never know when you are going to need help." I would come to appreciate that valuable lesson.

The death of someone close to me helped me see the need for this God that my mother talked about. As I began to learn more about the word of God I kept hearing how he wanted Christians to be blessed.

It wasn't until a couple of years ago I realized that everyone was blessed with hidden talents and gifts that if developed could give financial wealth beyond their dreams; not only financial wealth but happiness beyond their wildest imagination. I now realize that blessings and prosperity don't mean having it all for one's self.

God, I ain't trying to hear all that!

We must give to those who need us. In the end all that's really going to matter is what we gave others.

And do not forget to do good and share with others, for such sacrifices GOD is pleased (Hebrews 13:16, NIV)

Pastor Otis Lockett Sr. provided me with a comprehensive definition for success, but I also learned that you still have to go out and define what success is. I found it to be a journey that never stops.

The Definition of Success
1. Knowing GOD and what he desires for my life
2. Growing to my maximum potential
3. Sowing seeds to help others.

In knowing God and what he desires for my life, I figured out that He wants us to be successful in whatever we do. He wants us to dream and become more than we are.

May he give you the desires of your heart and make all your plans succeed (Psalms 20:4)

But even though God wants us to be successful, he doesn't want us to be successful apart from him. As sons and daughters of the true and living God, He wants us to achieve greatness because He (the greater one) made us, but He wants us to achieve by seeking a relationship with Him first.

Most of us have dreams of things we want to accomplish; things we want to do that we feel will make our lives more meaningful. We start out zealous and excited about the future, but something happens along the way. It never fails. I heard a speaker once say; "the definition of success is the ability to bear pain." I thought it was very silly at the time I heard it. What he meant was so much deeper than the words themselves. You see, successful people do what unsuccessful people are unwilling to do. In every instance this process is unforgiving. It is designed to weed out those who aren't ready to have success. It comes in the form of adversity. It is designed to make you quit and abandon your dreams. Adversity comes in many forms—maybe a failure or even a personal tragedy. Whatever form it comes in, it is designed to cause pain or discomfort.

My own journey has been cluttered with adversity, but I learned one thing after all the nights of tears and praying. Adversity has a lesson in which to be learned. God always has an opportunity there. Thus the endeavor is to go and find it.

My desire is to use the principles I've learned on my journey and share them with you. Sometimes we see the things we want as a state of bliss, almost like heaven. The reality is that sometimes getting to heaven means going through hell. However, the greatest joy comes in knowing that, through it all, God is there waiting for us to discover the successes he has planned for us.

CHAPTER ONE:

The Transition

Prayer, it's something that has been just as much a part of my life as breathing. My mother is a praying woman. I can still hear her on the phone and the way that unexpected outbursts of "thank you, Jesus!" or "Lord have mercy" would ring out throughout her conversations. Prayer is the staple that holds our family, as well as my mother, together. She is the type that prayed with people in the grocery store, on the phone, or wherever prayer was needed.

She always prayed with me, and while half the time I considered it routine, I expected and appreciated it. I didn't understand all of her actions, but there was a great respect and involuntary admiration for her and her beliefs. I recall us eating fried green tomatoes or fried sweet potatoes with sugar on top and talking. The crackle of the fryer was the drone that set the tone for our conversation. My mother is a strong woman with a big heart and just as beautiful on the outside as on the inside. My mother and I have kindred spirits, unquestionably. While I can't explain it, she *ALWAYS* knew what was going on in my life. She knew when I hurt, when I was excited, and when I was in trouble, regardless of whether I told her or not, including the time we robbed Mr. Smith's house.

Mr. Smith was a former pro ball player who owned a sporting goods store and kept inventory at his house. Two of my friends, Pless and Chris were both on the high school football team with me, and it was the summer before our senior season. Pless was a good athlete with a potentially bright future, but he had the tendency to make some silly decisions. He loved starting fights, seemed to be a magnet for trouble, and lacked overall mental stability. Chris, on the other hand was the type that lived for the moment. We had grown up together and been close ever since we were kids. While he had the talent to play anywhere, he didn't have the grades. It seemed that all he lived for was the moment.

While hanging out at Pless' house one day, his younger cousin came up with a plan to rob Mr. Smith. To this day I have no idea how he knew that Mr. Smith was out of town for the weekend. My job was simple; drop them off at the top of the hill and pick them up in the same spot twenty minutes later. I was stupid to even entertain the idea and even more stupid to consent. Those were the longest twenty minutes of my young life. All I could think of was getting caught. Would I go to jail? Would I be unable to graduate and go to college? I started to leave them more than once, but then I would've been a punk, even in my own eyes. All of these factors weighed on my mind. After my conscience had attacked me for twenty minutes, I was shaken. As the eternity ended, I saw shadows approaching the hill, then figures carrying trash bags full of merchandise. They had done it, but instead of feeling a sense of accomplishment, I was trying to persuade my heart not to jump out of my chest. This was against everything I had ever been taught and my body knew it. Chris and I took our share and went our way. The whole ride home Chris was telling me to "be cool" and "relax", but that was like asking someone without a tongue to talk. There was nothing he or anyone else could say that could calm me down. It was as if his statement brought out the police sirens. I nearly lost everything I had drunk since the day before. It was only after the police drove past us, apparently heading somewhere else, that my heart rate decreased and I began to think rationally again. The panic was over, but my fear was still alive. I had heard the wake up call.

When I arrived home I felt some comfort, but couldn't rest easy. As much as I love my mother, she was the last person I wanted to see. God told her things, she'd always told me. I begged Him to keep this one a secret and to trust that I might tell her in due time. That, or let her be asleep when I went inside. I was out of luck.

Of all the nights for my mother to be up sewing in the guestroom, this night was the worst. Guilt was undoubtedly written all over my face. I tried my best to play it off and direct our brief conversation to something casual. When I asked her why she was up so late, she replied that she couldn't sleep so she got up to make something. She never stayed up late. It was as if God had told on me without saying a word. She wanted me to come and talk but I refused, claiming that I was tired and sleepy. She insisted.

"Just for a few minutes," she said.

I was trapped and had no choice. As soon as I sat, she looked at me through those big, awkward glasses she always wore while sewing and asked me, "What's wrong?"

These were the last two words I wanted to hear, but the first two I had expected. Of course I tried to play it off, but my fear exposed me.

"I don't care what you say, something's wrong with you," she said.

I was forced to tell her the truth. I don't know whether it was God in my mother, my respect for her or both, but I could never lie to her. As I confessed, I was filled with pain for what I had done, but the truth also brought a release of sorts. I felt purged, even as I waited for what would come next.

My mother's expression never changed, so it was impossible for me to discern what she was thinking. This was the second eternity that I had experienced in the course of four hours. Finally, my mother spoke.

"Son, we didn't raise you like that and don't ever do anything like that again. Everything's gonna be all right."

And just like that, it was over. Though I'd felt God had betrayed me, I realized he'd had to in order for me to feel forgiven and for peace to be restored. My mother prayed with me then.

My father never knew, and would not have approved. He was a strong man with a lot of pride. His strength had always been phenomenal to me. Though he wasn't a big man, all 6'0, 170 pounds of his frame commanded respect. When he spoke, my friends and I listened. He was a top car salesman and had won everything from boats to lump sums of money, but he still wanted more. He especially resented working for people who didn't respect him. As a successful black man, he was often faced with the prejudice of white coworkers and employers.

"You'll still be a nigger to them regardless of what you do or accomplish", he said.

It was him who challenged me seriously about going to a predominantly black school, saying that the experience would be something that I would always remember and be proud of.

After making All-City, All-Conference, and All-Metro in football, I had plenty of options on where to go to school. It never crossed my mind to play for a black school. The glitz and glam would come from playing at a white school. After all, what black schools play on TV? What pro scouts visit black schools? What black school has ever had a chance of going to a bowl game and winning it all? In the midst of asking myself these questions, I realized that my subconscious mind had indeed been programmed to think that if something was white, it was better. That was a racist mentality and an unhealthy thought pattern. A&T would help prepare me for the obstacles of life while allowing me to be proud of who I was and my cultural roots.

My Arrival

As I've said, my mother was a praying woman. To her, prayer should be in every event in life, and my arrival to college was no exception. Upon arrival, just before my friend Stan and I got out of the van, my mother began to pray in that familiar voice. Her tone and my heart rate increased simultaneously with anticipation of what was about to happen in my life, matching the fervency of her prayers of protection. This was college; the four years that bridged the gap between adolescence and manhood.

It was 1983, and it was the beginning of the rest of my life. I really didn't know what to expect. I was the freshman recruit from Atlanta and while I knew that I was good enough to help take this team to the next level, I was still apprehensive. I had come here so that I could make a mark; anything else was considered failure.

The football team was a group of men from various backgrounds with one common goal— championships. Blue chips were few and far between on this squad, but hard work and determination were easy to find. I was convinced that no school had athletes that worked harder than we did. Not everyone could take the kind of practice that we went through every day, and many of the recruits were leaving. The upperclassmen were probably the worst ingredient in the whole situation. They constantly harassed the rest of us. I was determined to prove myself to them and everyone else before the season was over, even though some of them were punks anyway and hadn't impressed me on or off the field.

A&T was . . . different. The black college experience immediately gripped and affected me. The layout of the campus, the size of the dorm rooms; everything was different than what I had expected. I had been recruited by schools like Georgia Tech, schools that were predominantly white and would offer more exposure, but this school was different. Nothing could prepare me for the life lessons that I would learn. And being a football player immediately put me into a different cast of people. More was expected of me than of others and that was a two-edged sword. Even freshmen had groupies, but the level of stress to perform far outweighed the increased popularity. This was a transition; in high school I had been a big fish in a little pond, now I was a little fish in a big pond and it was time to sink or swim. I was used to respect; as a football player, I commanded it wherever I went. Here the upperclassmen, no matter how bad they were on the field, acted as if they were all that. It irked me to no end.

A&T had a culture all it's own, including some fine women. They came in all shapes and sizes. If you liked 'em tall and thick, short and petite, skinny or huge, there was something there for you. Along with the good, there was also the bad and the ugly. A good example of the bad was the three phones on our side of the dorm that had to be shared by fifty guys. If you did get a girl, there was no way for her to call you and get through, and calling her was pretty tough. The ugly was the food in the cafeteria and the bathroom set up. The cafeteria food was awful and the bathroom showers had no curtains and the toilets had no stalls. Combine all of these things plus the atmosphere of a black college and you've got life at A&T. Despite all of this, I loved being there.

Like all black colleges (I believe), the hobbies were of course, partying, hanging out in the union, and playing spades. My partner's name was Rico, and we had gotten so good that we would go from dorm to dorm whippin' folk's tails just to finance our late night snack at Kroger or Burger King. When we won the tournament that the Deltas put on, everyone was mad at us saying that we cheated, but we didn't care. They were a bunch of suckers as far as we were concerned and we laughed in their faces with the fifty dollars in prize money. Actually, it's ironic that we were partners because prior to that I disliked him. He was always trying to pull a fast one on somebody. In spite of that, I found a respect for him because he stood up for himself and had your back if you needed him.

When we weren't playing spades, we were either on the strip hanging out or getting ready for a function. The strip was the street that ran through the middle of campus, past our dorm (Cooper Hall), the student union, and the gym (Moore Gym). This was the spot to meet women and trip out with the fellas. "Function" was the word that we used for party. Ben from St. Louis would DJ and we would constantly have parties in the basement of our dorm. I had been to parties before, but the experience of a party on a black college campus is something that is unforgettable. The pulsating, loud music, the unbearable heat, and of course, the extremely fine women made for an exciting and unpredictable experience. There had to be at least eight girls for every one guy at A&T, and when they came out to the functions, the fellas were like kids in a candy store with a gift certificate.

All of these elements made up my home for the next four years. Every opportunity could also be a distraction, seeing that there were so many different things to do, so many responsibilities, and so many new people. The key was properly prioritizing things to be successful. Regardless of how many fine women I saw, I knew that my first priority was the books and my second priority was football; everything else was secondary. During my years there, I knew, not only would this be challenged, but I would have to dig deep into myself to find what I was made of. It was my first step towards the success I craved so much.

God, I ain't trying to hear all that!

CHAPTER TWO:

The Beginning

Football season was a time of celebration, school pride, and of course stress. We had been recruited to help turn a struggling team around. We had one goal in mind, to win a championship before our senior year was over, and we refused to stop at anything less. I knew how bad A&T had been the last couple years prior to my arrival, which I hoped would prove to be to my advantage. If I could help turn a struggling team into a perennial powerhouse, exposure might come.

In spite of the potential and supposed glamour of being a college football player, I was a freshman and the advantages were yet to show. I can still hear the coaches banging on the doors of our room at 5:45 a.m. and the profanity that followed if we failed to get up after their first call. I hated them for this. It seemed like just five minutes before that I had gone to sleep. "Get your butts up!" they would yell. If you failed, the coaches would literally come in your room, turn on the lights and scream at you at the top of their lungs until you got up. What an advantage I had being a college football player! I mean, sure the other students got to sleep an extra two to three hours, maybe more, and had less pressure on them to perform at the top of their game all the time, and sure we had a curfew that, if broken, meant suspension for various lengths of time, but I was a college football player. It took time, a lot of time, for me to see that going through all of this hell was really worth it.

As we would drag ourselves to the field house for morning practice, I often tried to decide what was worse, rolling around in the morning grass, which made you itch like crazy, or practicing in the afternoon when it was so humid you could taste the heat. After a while, I came to the conclusion that I hated them equally. Evidently I wasn't alone because people were quitting left and right. We all thought it would be easier, but some just couldn't take it. Most of the people that quit did it by not showing up for practice anymore, moving out of the dorm, or disappearing from the dorm while everyone else was asleep. I can't count the number of times that I was almost one of them, but there was something inside of me, I don't know if it was desire, pride, or fear, that kept me on the team. I knew that I could never live down quitting. Besides, the two-a-day practices could only last but so long, and the worst that could happen to me is I would pass out. In fact, one of our coaches had the same theory and would justify our continual running by stating, "You will pass out before you die!" and laughing. While I never shared in his humor, I just figured that if Stan, Los and Dee Bell could make it, so could I.

Stan was my homeboy from Atlanta that rode to school with me. We didn't get close until after high school graduation. Stan was a big dude and loved to eat. I mean, I love to eat too, but his appetite was violent. He loved fried chicken, especially Bojangles fried chicken, so much so that it became his new nickname. Stan would hide buckets of it under his bed so that no one would ask him for any. Though he was stingy with the food, Stan had a big heart. Chicken was the only thing that he wouldn't give you his last of. Many times during our freshman year, it seemed like Stan wasn't really into football. In fact, there were a couple of times that I had to talk him out of quitting. If he could stick with it, feeling that way, so could I.

Another source of influence to me was Carlos. Carlos, or "Los," was a fat dude from Detroit who, just like us, came to camp out of shape. Los, Stan and I would hang out looking for all-you-can-eat joints. Los was the type that took no junk from the upperclassmen, and that I respected. They said that he looked like a fat Yoda from Star Wars, and said that the fat rolls on his side looked like change machines, so they called him quarters, nickels, and dimes. Though he occasionally got mad, his usual response was, "I don't care, cause can't none of y'all whip my tail," (though his choice of direct objects was a bit different and more profane). Despite all of the upperclassmen's junk talking, none of them tried to prove him wrong, which was a sign of respect. Los might have taken a lot of teasing, but people respected him. His attitude earned him that. It was a point I would always remember.

Though Los was huge, Dee Bell was the largest human being I had ever met personally. He stood 6'6, weighed 385 pounds, and during practice, his eyes would get blood-shot red. I was sure that he was going to have a heart attack or a stroke from being so big and having to do so much running. Dee Bell was a fierce competitor and hated losing. Other guys would try to take advantage of his lack of speed because he was so big, but he was smart and could use his weight to his advantage. During practice, we used to do a drill called the "OKI" drill. This drill pits the offensive and defensive player one-on-one against each other. It was extremely violent and players either got hurt and humiliated, or earned respect and reverence. One day a cat named Poteat challenged Dee Bell in OKI. Poteat was from Virginia and his high school had won multiple state championships. Because he was big like Dee Bell, he felt like he could take him. In the midst of destroying his confidence, Dee Bell also ruptured a disc in Poteat's back, forcing him to sleep on his dresser because his bed was so uncomfortable. That humiliation earned Poteat the nickname "Big Weak Poteat," and eventually he quit the team. Pride, peer pressure and acceptance can be a huge motivational factor.

God, I ain't trying to hear all that!

Misconceptions

Misconceptions can destroy confidence and kill motivation. Before I came to A&T, I had formed a preconceived notion on how life would be, how football would be, and most of all, how I would be. Being from Georgia and receiving so many awards, I figured that I would instantly be great and a cut above other players. Georgia was considered by many to be the fourth-best state for high school football behind Florida, Texas and California. I quickly came to realize that I was a dime a dozen player for A&T, and that in order to be special I was going to have to do some very special things. Everyone that was on the team was "All everything." My dad had always told me that I was just as good as the next guy, but he also said that you had to work twice as hard to be recognized as half as good, regardless of how good you really were.

In high school, football players were always the big men on campus. Even if you were a freshman, if you were recognized as a great ball player, the upperclassmen would jock you (especially the ladies). My girlfriend, Michelle, was my high school sweetheart. This was a woman I loved so much so that I cried two days before leaving. I thought that nothing could separate us; however, I was warned by my man, Russell, a couple of weeks before I left. He told me that if I had a girl, I might as well let her go because I was going to see women that could sever the strongest of relationship ties. I told him he was crazy. He simply said, "You'll see." How prophetic his words turned out to be.

When I got to A&T I thought that the girls would instantly love me and the guys would idolize me. These girls were some of the finest honeys that I had ever seen. All shapes, all sizes, all styles, whatever your flavor (French Vanilla, Butter Pecan, or Double Dutch Chocolate), there was the top of the line for you to look at and attempt to sample. Although I had a girl in Atlanta, I was like a kid in a candy store, but with no money because none of them seemed to recognize me. How right my friend Russell had been.

Russell had been a senior ballplayer at Tennessee State University. They tried to use him to recruit me. When I decided to go to A&T, he was a little disappointed but he still wanted me to succeed so he advised me all that he could. The best advice that he gave me was telling me to never forget that it wasn't going to be easy. Standing on the balcony of the dorm and watching these women go by showed me that his prophecy was true.

Grades were never an issue in high school for star football players. Because teachers were interested in the success of the football team, they were willing to do whatever was necessary to insure that academics didn't become a hindrance. I never worried about whether or not I was in danger of failing. Coaches and teachers always looked out with extra help or exemptions from certain responsibilities when necessary. Mind you, I was a good student regardless. I graduated with honors from high school and was a hard worker. However, that extra support kept me from experiencing a lot of the pressure that the average student experienced.

I loved the fact that in college none of the classes met every day. Classes met Monday, Wednesday, and Friday, or Tuesday and Thursday. With some good planning it was possible to get a schedule with an entire day off. I remember the first day that I walked into one of my biology classes. The instructor told us point blank that some of the people in the class would fail. Though I didn't want it to be me, reality caught up with me when I saw the curriculum and course outline and I knew that I was in for a struggle. I had heard that at HBCU the instructors cared about you and the classes were smaller for an atmosphere more conducive for learning. How could this clown care about me? The first thing that comes out of his mouth is that there would definitely be some failures in his class. His theory of motivation was very questionable.

I even had an English teacher, Dr. Furgeson, who suggested that I quit football to apply myself more to my studies. She would tell me that I was a good student, but that I needed to work harder. She saw quitting the team as the only viable option. She had to be crazy; football was the main reason I came to the school and she wanted me to give that up? I remember working for hours on a paper and getting a C- on it. In any other class that would have been a disappointment, but in her class I was proud of that grade. She challenged me to think and be creative in ways that I had never been challenged before. Though there were times when I wrote essays over and over and while my grade never got better, she applauded my efforts. Dr. Furgeson was a stern, intelligent, and caring woman who weeded out students who weren't serious about learning. Students would avoid her like the plague and by mid-semester there were usually only ten to twelve students left in her class.

Everything was wrong. My thoughts about my status, my teachers, my classes, even myself. I was forced to work harder than I had ever worked and circumstances were testing my theories about how good I really was. By the end of the semester, the picture came into full focus when my GPA was 1.4 out of a possible 4.0. I had no clue how this could possibly have happened. Then I realized the power of denial. Things change around you constantly, but as long as you deny change and think that everything is the same, you get left behind. Procrastination and wrong priorities had a huge price tag.

Life as a Player . . .

Successful people don't rely on lucky breaks; they make their own. Most of the time those of us on the football team were just trying to make it from day to day. Still, I felt that those who took the easy road out by quitting would regret it in the future, no matter how much they thought they were dodging a bullet now.

We were constantly dogged by the upperclassmen and the coaches were extremely hard on us. Our head coach, Coach Mo Forte, was the worst of them all. It took some time for me to get used to his hard-nosed style of coaching and discipline. When he came to my house to recruit me, he'd seemed like one of the nicest men that I had ever met. He told my mother how he would be like a father to me, guaranteed that I would get in no trouble, and insured that all of my needs would be supplied and that he would bring out the best in me. Whatever. Of course, in retrospect I see the benefits and lessons learned from playing for him and I can appreciate it, but then? Then was a different story. The first day I stepped into camp, he was like Dr. Jekyl and Mr. Hyde. He went from this self-proclaimed father figure to this anal-retentive that took his personal problems out on his players. If we weren't a bunch of fat-asses, then we were dumb-asses that looked like horse or dog crap (his choice of words were a bit different).

I understand motivating players to be all that they can be, but he took it a little too far. Once he even told a guy that his body was so fat and ugly, he didn't see how he was going to get a girl. That made me mad. I knew that if he was this mean to him, he was bound to say something like that to me. The thought of him humiliating me in front of my teammates was very upsetting.

He was hard on me because I'd received so much praise coming out of high school, and he didn't feel that I lived up to expectations. That was because I came to camp out of shape. In my mind, I thought that I would be able to succeed off of sheer ability. There is no skill or profession in life that formula works in. Forte taught me that I was going to have to work for anything that I wanted in life.

He had come from bigger schools like the University of Minnesota and Michigan State, and knew what it took to win. He sported a huge Big Ten Championship ring that he received at Michigan State when he was an assistant coach there. His goal was to bring that same excellence to A&T. Whenever I saw that ring, it motivated me. I wanted one, too. What I wasn't ready for was the process of getting it.

Success comes to those who deserve it. The work ethics that I learned playing football helped me in every aspect of life. Those deserving success are those that are willing to work hard to get what they want. Coach Forte and the other coaches would constantly say, "leave it on the field." I didn't figure out what it meant until the end of my freshman year. They meant to give it all that you had each time out, even when you didn't feel like it.

Throughout life I've learned that you can better yourself by noting someone else's mistakes and shortcomings, then removing them from your life. I learned one of these lessons from Coach Forte as well. He was candid, arrogant, and many times unreasonable. Saying he wasn't a people person was an understatement. He approached everyone: his players, his coaches and administration, in a harsh and insensitive manner. Administration, I could understand. They always seemed to slow the process of the football team getting what we needed, whether it was new equipment to getting the bus fixed when it broke down. What I didn't like was the way he treated his coaching staff. These were the men that in essence made or broke his career. He needed them to help achieve success and reach his goals.

I particularly hated how he treated Coach E. His real name was Jack Eatinger. He was our offensive line coach and treated all of the players with respect and caring. He was a soft-spoken dude until you pissed him off. Though he and Forte both pushed us hard, we knew that he cared for us, even beyond football. He gave each lineman individual attention, and let us know that he loved us, from the best to the worst. While we never showed our appreciation externally and sentimentally, everyone knew how everyone else felt.

Coach Forte was a competitor who hated to lose and liked everything his way on his time. This was understandable because he was the head coach, but I always expected Coach E to go off on him. Forte would often curse him out in front of the players about various things, including hotel reservations not being ready or if he hadn't gotten film from the other team yet. Respect is key in any organization, especially the players or subordinates respecting their leader. When the respect element is fragmented, then there will be problems in the organization. Because of Forte's lack of respect, many of the players began to disrespect Coach E. The influence and example of a leader can make or break a group or team.

Game Time . . .

The closer it got to our first game, the more things seemed to change. The regular students came back and all you could hear was music thumping from cars driving by. Most of the fellas on campus either admired or envied you, and many of the girls wanted to get with you. This is what I was expecting when I was in high school preparing for college. The campus was buzzing with excitement for our first game. It was against Winston-Salem State, and they were our biggest rivals. It was gratifying that people appreciated us as athletes, but the season would show just how fickle people were. As long as we won we were the greatest, but whenever we lost we were the worst team on the planet.

I hadn't eaten or hardly slept the night before, and when we walked into Grove Stadium for the game I had butterflies in my stomach. I had never played in a stadium that big before. I mean, don't get me wrong, I had played before some crowds, but there were 40,000 people in the stands for this game. Grove Stadium was the home of Wake Forest's football team. Though Winston-Salem State was the home team, their stadium couldn't hold the expected crowd.

I remember when Coach E called for me to go into the game. It was like time stood still. My heart was thumping like I had stolen something. I was so nervous, not from fear of the other players, but that I was going to mess up and let my team down. True courage is putting your fears behind you and doing what you have to do. I didn't have much that day.

On my first college play, I was so concerned with what I was going to do that I did nothing.

When the quarterback gave the cadence to start the play, I reacted late. By the time I moved I ended up running into my own running back and tackling him. The other team's players were laughing at me and my teammates cursed at me. Two plays later I was back on the sidelines. It was a humbling experience. I was the big time recruit from Georgia, but evidently I didn't know when to start a play, or worse, which player to block.

We ended up losing that game. Actually, we ended up losing a lot of games. To put it frankly, we were sorry. We were so sorry that people considered playing us to be a bye week where you picked up a win. I know that this was hard on the upperclassmen. Nevertheless, they played every game like we were going to the national playoffs. They never quit and always played the full 60 minutes. Amazingly, this losing, especially with these seniors, taught me something. Their level of commitment was the key to winning. Even though we weren't winning then, until we got their level of heart and commitment, we were never going to. Though they must have been discouraged with the fact that we were losing the way we were, they never showed it. They would always get mad at us freshmen, but we took it as a source of motivation.

Jesse Britt was a perfect example. He was a big yet fast country boy that was always joking and smiling, but he was a beast on the football field. He would knock you out, then help you up when you regained consciousness. I liked him because he was humble, but got the job done. When he got on us for not giving it our all, it was because he truly cared.

When you're losing there's a lot of finger pointing and blaming going on. The coaches would blame the upperclassmen for lack of leadership. The upperclassmen blamed the freshmen for lack of heart. The freshmen blamed everyone for not understanding. The bottom line was that we were so busy beating ourselves that we couldn't beat anyone else.

I believe that at times animosity was purposely created between the players by the coaches. Since we were all freshmen, respect was the name of the game. We tried to kill each other every day to get it and make a good impression.

Regardless of how big, fast, or highly recruited, we were all on the same playing field and looked at in the same way: as freshmen. I remember this one freshman named Ernest Riddick. He was only 5'8", but he was one of the meanest people I had ever met. He would hit you even if you were down just to send a message that nothing was going to come without a price. His nickname was "doom." He carried it with him from high school. Though he was a freshman, there were upperclassmen that were afraid of him and I couldn't understand it. He and I fought almost everyday. I never believed that you had to win every fight to get respect, you just had to be willing to fight.

I used to think he was a little off because he never smiled and always had a look of pain on his face. Ironically, he was a nice guy off the field. He would always offer me chicken and ribs when he returned from his home visits (he was from Edenton, NC, a small town just off the coast). It was strange that he came to school with almost nothing. All that was in his room was his record player with a tape deck that looked about 20 years old. He always listened to the Isley Brothers and only slept under one sheet, even in the winter. He didn't bring a lot of clothes with him and his room looked like no one lived there. He showed me that material possessions weren't the driving force in everyone's life. All he wanted to do was win, and though we did very little of that our first year, we had three years left and we vowed that things would get better.

God, I ain't trying to hear all that!

CHAPTER THREE:

Tradition

Tradition is a funny thing. Some traditions are good and serve as staples in various communities and groups, but others need their validity questioned. Many times there are pointless traditions that we follow without ever asking ourselves why we do what we do. Traditions can also hold the key to the future and create a sense of camaraderie.

For instance, on our college campus there was a big tree everyone called the tree of knowledge. At first I had no idea why they called it that. Maybe somebody had one too many and started kickin' some kind of knowledge or philosophy and thus gave the tree's name birth. It was just a big tree right in front of our dorm that all the ball players hung out under to look at the honeys, drink a few brews, or just shoot the breeze.

Ironically, it was the tree of knowledge that housed all of us that skipped class for the day.

Regardless of whatever stigma was attached to the tree, we felt like this was our home. Obviously, others did too. It was an unwritten law that if you weren't a football player or friends with one, then you didn't hang under the tree, no questions asked. This was a tradition that was respected and accepted by all. The tree served as a gathering spot, but more importantly it was a place that we could go to when we weren't feeling up to par, or wanted to share some great news. After leaving college it dawned on me why it was named the tree of knowledge. The tree was a place that we could share our feelings and insights; a place that opened up communication and allowed us to explore the experiences and mindset of others. It was this location that allowed us to get the answers to life that we all so desperately needed. Being young adults we acted like we knew it all, but deep down inside we were all in search of answers.

There were other traditions that I wasn't so fond of.

Greasing

Greasing was the art of beating a man to test his manhood, no more, no less. As a "dumb freshman", I had often heard the term, but didn't really know what it meant, and didn't care. I would come to find out. I would also learn how damaging this type of tradition could be.

God, I ain't trying to hear all that!

One day Coach Forte gave us the afternoon off from practice, so me and my man, CeCe, decided to go and beat some of the upperclassmen in spades. CeCe was from Melbourne, Florida. He was a big, dark-skinned dude that wore a doo-rag on his head all the time. He was always joking with or about you, but he was an animal on the football field. We formed a strong friendship because we both had such a strong passion for football and loved to play spades, as did so many other athletes on our team.

CeCe tried to play spades every time he could and didn't like losing, making us a perfect fit. Not to mention the fact that he was a master bluffer and most of the upperclassmen liked him. I was the exact opposite. The upperclassmen hated me because I was from Atlanta, highly recruited, and Forte let everyone know it. This was one of his ways of creating animosity among his players and weeding out the weak. I talked trash to most of them and didn't respect them because they didn't impress me at all. To them, I was all talk because I hadn't proven myself. Spades was our way to regain respect we might have lost in practice. It was routine for me to take a man's money in spades. Losing wasn't in my vocabulary. Spades became a refuge for me in the sense that it was my ace-in-the-hole to gain respect. CeCe and I were determined to get respect either on the field or by taking money from the other players.

CeCe and I went to Ken Brown and Kennedy Marshall's room. Larry Taylor and Marion Haywood were in there as well. All of these guys played on the offensive line with me, so I interacted with them daily. CeCe and I didn't think much about it, except for the fact that this was an opportunity to whip all of them and talk major noise.

We began winning, and we began to gloat over the victories. Pretty soon, the conversation got heated and became personal. All of a sudden, I heard a click. Haywood had locked the door. I didn't know what was going to happen. All of a sudden, Marshall grabbed me with his big southern fried, country twanged arms.

"You think you tough? We gon' see!"

The rest of them hit me like a tidal wave and began pulling off my pants. I began to kick and punch whoever was in range. Eventually I got tired and my efforts to fight back left and they pulled off my pants. As I resisted, they got ripped in the process. They started pouring after-shave and lotion on my butt and slapped it repeatedly. They must have hit me 30 to 40 times but it felt like an eternity. Part of it was to teach me a lesson, and part of it was tradition, some kind of test of manhood. This was the stupid, pointless tradition that I hated not only because of my bruised ego, but because of the potential for real injury.

I know that I wasn't the only one hurting; I kicked a couple of them in the stomach and in the face, but by then it didn't matter. I felt like crying, but I refused to let them see any weakness. I was pretty sure that I was the first one to get greased that year.

God, I ain't trying to hear all that!

"All y'all just a bunch of punks and faggots!" I yelled out trying to gain some redemption.

I heard Brown tell me to shut up before they did it again. All I could say was "Yeah right," hoping that they wouldn't. I was humiliated to say the least. When we got back to the room, I lit into CeCe.

"You could've helped me!" I screamed.

"What was I going to do with all of them?" he said. "We would've both gotten killed then!"

Though I was still mad, I knew he was right. I just didn't want to be the only one humiliated. Later in life, I could look back and see that this was a tradition that should have been questioned. For both those who got through it well, and those who didn't, there were lifelong repercussions.

Not too long after that the upperclassmen started greasing all of the freshmen on the hall. I was surprised at the lack of solidarity among the freshmen. It seemed to me that they would band together and fight back, but the rite of passage and acceptance among the seniors was more important than any togetherness or common sense. Most of the freshmen knew it was coming and just wanted to get it over with.

One guy named Big Jones just pulled his pants down and let them grease him with no resistance. He was 6'4, 290 pounds, as strong as a bull and could've easily defended himself with some success. His willingness to roll over and submit was shocking. Upperclassmen lost respect for him and considered him an outcast. They felt he didn't value the tradition. Looking back I realized he understood its importance, but felt that it was stupid just like everyone else. His lack of involvement sent out a signal that it was time for change. He was questioning the validity of a pointless and even dangerous tradition.

There were others that were willing to do anything not to get greased, and many times those instances became very dangerous. One freshman named Tibadeux hit an upperclassman in the head with a blunt object trying to avoid getting greased. The upperclassman needed stitches to close up the wound. Most of the fights happened when a freshman would call an underclassman out, but that never stopped greasing. The funny thing about tradition is that while you go through it you despise it, but when you look in retrospect, many traditions are embraced. Many will blindly follow what has gone before, even when it might put some in danger.

By my sophomore year, I had resolved to never grease a freshman while I was in college. Nevertheless, within two months I was talking of greasing like it was the next best thing to my mom's sweet potato pie. Even though I didn't forget the pain and humiliation that I went through, I didn't care. Somehow, I had come to forget my conviction in the face of inflicting on someone else what I had been forced to endure. All we were doing was practicing hazing, the same thing that the fraternities and sororities practiced. These traditions were not only painful, they were dangerous.

Some fraternities would beat people unconscious or cause profuse bleeding all in the name of brotherhood. One guy named Clemente almost died when he was struck in the head with a 2x4 piece of wood. He ended up having to have brain surgery. Another guy lost hearing in one of his ears from being struck on that side of his head. My understanding was that most people on that particular line suffered some sort of injury.

To my surprise, some of the sororities were just as bad as the fraternities. I remember a friend of mine was pledging, and obviously because of this she didn't speak to me when she saw me on campus. When I went to visit her in her room, she told me with a terrified look that I had to leave. While we were talking we heard someone coming. She told me to hide in the closet. Soon after, three girls came in and began to verbally abuse her about something that she didn't do. When she responded, one of the girls punched her in the chest because she wasn't satisfied with her answer. When I saw my friend bend over in obvious pain, I wanted to jump out of the closet and whip them like two dudes, but I couldn't. My friend would've never forgiven me. I was so mad. I wondered how she could allow someone to disrespect her like that and act as if it was nothing. Because of her desire to be a sorority member she was willing to take constant abuse.

These desires pollute your sense of right and wrong. Fraternities and sororities are built on the idea of respect and play a vital role in many communities and campuses, but a few individuals can destroy the integrity of the organization. Little did I know I was subjected to the same thing and doing it to others. Tradition can cause you to become blind to the real meaning. When people want something badly enough, they are willing to take or do anything, and that is not always good. It is the mere act of tradition that seems to hold them in check, the need to fit in with their peers, and those who have gone before.

When I asked my friend about what she endured, she simply replied, "You wouldn't understand. Everyone has to go through it. They all went through it." After she finally got accepted and was able to wear her colors, I asked her, was it worth going through all that she went through? She said "No!" which is what I figured.

It's hard to turn to your brother and sister to pick you up, when they are the ones that knock you down. Traditions such as this take a system of support and turn it into a system of fear and danger. All we really wanted was to just be accepted. We were willing to endure anything in name of belonging.

Joning

"Joning," or what we sometimes called "clowning," was another pastime that we used to do just that: pass time. It was the act of ridiculing or belittling someone in the presence of others to bring about humiliation. Anything and everything about a person was fair game. It stressed a person's imperfections, and provided scores of entertainment until you were the person being clowned.

God, I ain't trying to hear all that!

Someone had gotten everyone started calling me "Be mine," short for "Be My Valentine," because they said my butt looked like a heart. I still don't know what they were doing looking at my butt. People would holler that all the way across campus.

I wasn't that great at joning, so for the most part, I kept my mouth shut. I don't know what's worse, being joned on or trying to come back with something that wasn't close to being funny. To be good you had to be a quick thinker and have strong emotions. Once you got started it could go on for hours, depending on how many people crowded around to hear it. You would have a person that would laugh at something that wasn't even funny just to keep the contest going.

Once, Mozell and Johnnie Coleman went at it for what seemed to be all night. I laughed so hard that my side hurt for the whole next day. Johnnie was a well-liked country boy that some said looked like ET because of his head. In spite of this he was good at jonin'. He got respect because he was a good ball player. Though he was small in stature, he could hit as hard as the 300-pounders and he hated losing in anything, whether it was football or jonin'. He would tear a brother apart with that country accent and have everybody laughing at you. Some people would see him on campus and laugh because of the ET thing, but you could never tell whether or not it bothered him because he was always nice, so nice that people overlooked his head. Johnnie taught me a lot, whether he knew it or not. He showed me that what was on the inside would always outshine what was on the outside.

Everyone on the football team had a nickname during the jonin' season, particularly the freshmen. For example, some of the nicknames were:

Big Weak Poteat because he was a big guy with no strength.

Bojangles because he would always eat buckets of Bojangles chicken.

Doo Doo throat because his breath was always a little less than desirable.

Michelin Man because of the rolls of fat around his waist.

Blue because he was exceptionally dark-skinned.

Meatloaf because the guy had rolls of fat all around his neck.

Gazoo because he looked like the cartoon character.

While a lot of guys took jonin to heart, Judas, Jute for short, just let it roll off of him. He was a friendly guy that always wore a smile. I first noticed him when he came in late to a meeting that the freshmen players had with the coaching staff. One of the upperclassmen started calling him "Bertha", short for "Bertha Butt Boogie" because his butt was big. I still don't understand the football team's fascination with butts. Anyway, Jut and I became friends. He was a bold, sincere guy that wasn't afraid to talk to the girls. His personality was magnetic. When they would jone' on him, he would simply grin and say, "that stuff doesn't bother me," and keep kickin'. Soon the joke was that we were brothers and he got my portion of butt by mistake when we were born. Yet again, I learned from a friend a better way to react to a situation. Jut taught me that to let things roll was better than fighting them, or letting them affect your outlook.

Jonin' was a part of our college culture. Things on campus, or for that matter anywhere, remain the same. In every inner circle there is some type of "jonin." Simply put, it is another way for us as people to express our wit and creativity in a joking manner.

Traditions can be good. They can give us insight into the future and into the past, but they must always be questioned for validity before things get out of hand. That is why it is so important to question and challenge what has been going on for so long. If you don't seek to understand the meaning behind the tradition you will become programmed and continue the same cycle of humiliation and fear to gain respect.

God, I ain't trying to hear all that!

CHAPTER FOUR:

Relationships

Relationships are one of the greatest educational tools in life. Dealing with people not only teaches you about them, but it also teaches you about yourself. A great part of my learning came from my dating experiences.

When I first got to college, I thought that status was more important than personality. I thought that women wanted a man that could make them look better in the eyes of others more than they wanted one that would make them feel good about themselves. We men were like kids in a candy store with an appetite that couldn't be satisfied by one woman. By my junior year I realized that not everything that looked good was necessarily good for you.

As an athlete I saw all kinds of women, and because we were ball players we had our pick of the bunch. Our biggest competition for women was the basketball team. Even though I had a girlfriend at home, I wanted to experience some of the "treats" that were at the school. Besides, my girl at home was beginning to put subtle pressure on me concerning marriage, and at the time I wanted no part of that. I didn't even have money for the basic necessities of life like food, clothes, or toiletries. How was I going to take care of a wife? And honestly, I was really beginning to enjoy the college life.

It was like a game of cat and mouse. If you played the game right, you got your pick in the candy store. If not, you just had a sweet tooth that couldn't be satisfied. By this time, I had become roommates with Judas, who got along so well with the women, that I had the opportunity to benefit from his "magnetic personality." Even though I was from Atlanta (also known as Hotlanta) and was used to seeing beautiful women, I wasn't prepared for the number of good-looking women that were there at college. They came in all shapes and sizes.

My first two years I didn't really play the field because I was shy and had a girlfriend at home, but by my junior year I was really feeling the pressure. I had a friend at home, Russell, who had cautioned me before going to college how hard it would be to maintain relationships from high school. "If you've got a girlfriend," he warned, "drop her." His words bothered me at first, but I came to understand he was speaking from personal experience. By my junior year I wasn't as sweet on my high school sweetheart as I'd once been.

The Rules of the Game

Judas was determined to get me out to meet some honeys. He had a special way with the fairer sex. He would often bring girls to our room and I would have to leave so that they could be alone. Sex seemed to be the whole objective of relationships in college. Judas, seeing that my relationship back home was falling apart, became determined to hook me up with other women.

We started spending more and more time together, and I watched in amazement as women flocked to Judas. At first I didn't see the connection. I thought they were looking for status, but my roommate had the secret. He was sincere and connected with them emotionally. This was a revelation to me. I realized that this was a key. If a man could connect with a woman on an emotional level, other aspects became secondary. The ugliest guy in the world could pull a fly honey if he knew how to act and what to say. Judas would talk sweet to them, make them laugh, and most importantly, listen. The goal was to convince them that he was interested in more than sex, even if he wasn't. He was bold and unashamed because he didn't fear rejection. He understood that there were 500 fine women for each one that told him no, and he liked his odds.

After a while chasing women became an addiction. The better I got at pulling honeys the more I did it. Judas' boldness began to rub off on me. Surprisingly, it wasn't the sex that drove me but the chase and the challenge. There was something about the challenge of pulling a beautiful woman that tested you as a man and told you something about your ability. Because of this motivation, rejection didn't carry as much weight. However, there were some things that began to bother me about this approach.

A lot of times guys would lie about their intentions in the relationship. I often thought, "what if that was my sister or mother in college and a man lied to her just for sex?" It changed not only my perspective, but also my pursuit. I stopped lying to women about what I wanted in a relationship and became straightforward.

Playing the Game

Playing the game teaches you that there are consequences to every decision that you make, and they aren't always good. I remember getting up one morning to use the bathroom and noticing something wrong. There was a green, milky substance all over the front of my underwear. I didn't pay attention to it until I tried to use the bathroom. It was the worst feeling that I had ever experienced. There was an intense burning sensation and it felt like there were razors inside of me trying to come out when I urinated. I had been burned. When I found out that being burned and gonorrhea were one in the same, I got nervous. This was a sexually transmitted disease.

I started to ask questions about it. I targeted guys that I suspected had experienced the same problem. I tried to ask them without tipping them off to my own situation. The first thing that they said was, "You've been burned, ain't you?" I'd lie and say no, that I was just curious, but they knew. When I told Judas, he laughed and said that I had better go to the clinic immediately. Playing with fire meant that you would surely get burned. And yes, the pun was intended.

In every game there are setbacks and injuries. I had missed football games due to injuries or conditions and had to deal with them if I planned on playing again. And so it was in the game of relationships. The problem was how did I deal with this injury without letting on to everyone else what had happened?

I wasn't about to go to the school infirmary for fear of seeing someone I knew. I decided to go to the public infirmary. This way I could keep my situation on the down low and not damage my reputation. Apparently half the school had the same idea. I saw all kinds of students there, and we were all there for the same reason. I guess the only comforting thing was that they couldn't clown me because they were in the same boat.

The more I participated in this game, the more I realized that there were more negatives than positives. There were more people getting hurt than anything else, both guys and girls. Girls saw it as more than just sex; there was an emotional attachment that usually meant that for them, the relationship ended in pain. While I was still out to win, I tried to treat each lady with respect. I guess that was my way of justifying things. This was a game, and like any other game there were injuries, disappointments, and casualties. I didn't understand until adulthood the affects that my actions could have on these young ladies, and with my understanding came some regret.

While I can't change the past, I can help other men and women not make the same mistakes that I did. God only knows how many women have a low level of self-esteem and self worth because of past experiences with a selfish and insensitive man. Men who constantly treat women with no dignity or respect will have them feeling like less than a person, less than beautiful, all in the name of lust. Lust is insatiable and can lead to an unappeasable appetite for sex and attention. If you don't control lust it will control you until it destroys you.

We All Need More

I had become very tired of this cat and mouse relationship game. Regardless of the amount of different women that I had been with, there was still an emptiness inside. I realized I wasn't being to true to myself. I was acting just like all the other guys that I despised. I still hadn't broken up with my girlfriend at home. By lying to her, I was ultimately destroying her and any friendship we had. I made a decision to break it off and change my life.

I wanted more than just sex; I wanted companionship. I knew that there was something more to relationships than what I had experienced so far. I also understood that giving in to this emotion would probably make others think that I wasn't macho, but I didn't care.

There were things that could keep me occupied where I didn't have to focus on this overwhelming desire. One night I was in my room bored, just hanging out in the dorm. I didn't want to call any girls because I knew where that would lead. I was tired of just sex. I would only want them to leave afterward, and I didn't like that feeling. For the most part the dorm was empty. Almost everyone had left to go out for the night. There were a few of us who stayed back to play spades, listen to music and drink some beer. While combing the other rooms to see if I could possibly assemble a spades game, I ended up in Juan Jackson's room. He wasn't there, but there were two cute females in there dancing and laughing. As soon as I heard them talk I guessed that they were from somewhere up north, maybe New York or New Jersey. They told me their names were Deborah and Teresa, and that they were students at Bennett College (the all girls' school across the street). They were both from Long Island. They were small girls, but they were full of personality and though they weren't sisters they acted like it.

Teresa captivated me from the get go. She had an hourglass figure, her teeth were white and perfect, and her skin was a smooth pecan tan. But the kicker was her personality. I had never met a woman like her up to that point. There was only one problem, she was Juan's girlfriend. Though I had envisioned her with me, it was taboo among football players to try to talk to a teammate's girl.

The chitchat was basic until Juan came back from using the phone. When he came back, Teresa asked me if I could stay. I wasn't sure if that was a hint that she was attracted to me, but I told her that I had to leave because there were some things that I had to do. I had never been so tempted to try to take a friend's girl, but I put the team before myself. We didn't need any internal conflict right now.

For months I thought about her, but I made sure the thought quickly passed. I would see her and Juan every now and then, and made sure I kept on walking. One day while Juan and I were together I happened to ask him about her. To my surprise he seemed displeased with the relationship. My ears perked up. He asked me about Vera, a girl that I had occasionally dated but had mostly a physical relationship with. We didn't have much, conversations were minimal, and I would have given it up in a minute for a shot at Teresa. When I told him that things weren't going well, he jokingly suggested that we switch girls. I knew he was serious and it caught me off guard. I tried not to let my excitement at the prospect show. I suggested interest in the possibility. It's amazing that we thought we could control the lives of two other people without them knowing.

Based on what he was saying, Teresa wasn't giving him the sex that he wanted. That was fine with me because it spoke of her character. Within a month at least half of his suggestion was coming to pass; I saw him walking with Vera down the sidewalk, holding her hand. Teresa saw it too. The situation was becoming ideal for me to try and step in. I had to find a way to get in her path without being obvious. I would periodically ask Juan about her, but he said he didn't know and didn't care. He said he heard she was dating some rich dude from New York. I knew the guy Juan was talking about. He wore a lot of gold and drove a nice car. I knew I couldn't compete with the material things he had and I was going to have to rely on my personality. I wanted to make the dream of dating her become a reality. I had to do something.

I slowly developed a relationship with one of Teresa's friends named Regina. She was from up north and said whatever was on her mind. I would ask questions about Teresa, like whether or not she was dating someone. Her reply was always that she wasn't seeing anyone of significance. I was hoping that she would suggest the two of us meeting and hooking up, but she never did. Finally I decided to take the first step. Whatever happened would just happen. It was near the end of school and I knew that I had to do something or I was going to get nothing.

I told Regina that I was interested in Teresa and asked her what she thought my chances were. She got excited and volunteered to talk to her on my behalf. I didn't see or hear from Regina for a couple of weeks. I was on pins and needles. When I was finally able to ask her about Teresa's response she didn't answer the question, but told me to be in front of the cafeteria the next day between 5:00 and 6:00 p.m. She said that was around the time Teresa and her friend Deborah came through our campus going to Summit Ave.

God, I ain't trying to hear all that!

Just like Regina had said, at about 5:30 I saw Teresa walking my way. Regina had come to kind of make the connection. Surprisingly she was with my friend Judas! He realized what I was doing and grinned at me. It was the toughest thing in the world for me to act like I just happened to be there. Regina introduced me. Teresa remembered me from Juan's room and she began to smile. My insides were jumping. This was my big chance, the chance that I had been waiting on for months. All I had to do was ask her out or ask for her number and all of my fantasies could become realities.

I couldn't do it. I said that it was good to see her and I hoped to see her again. As soon as she left, Regina lit into me. How could I put her through all the trouble of hooking this up only to get scared? I gave her every excuse I could come up, but the bottom line was that I was scared.

Fear is a disease that has robbed countless people of destiny and opportunity. Excuses kill any opportunity that you have for a second chance. The window of opportunity doesn't stay open long, and it's up to us to jump through it when we can. Each window is a defining moment in determining our future. Now, it seemed like my window with Teresa had shut. Fear had robbed me of my chance, but if my window of opportunity had closed, I was determined to reopen it.

The Next Year

Football practice began and school followed soon after it. During the second week of school I saw Regina. We talked for a minute, asking each other about the summer. Then I got to the point. Had Teresa come back to school? It was obvious to her that I hated the opportunity that I'd missed and that I wanted another chance. She told me that Teresa was in the dorm. Though reluctant, she hooked it for me and got me her number.

Teresa and I talked for a couple of weeks, and I finally got her to agree to meet me before I left for our game in Philly against Delaware State. It was Heaven. I could have talked to her all night long, but I had to go. We agreed to meet again the Monday after the game.

All during the trip I thought about her and listened to slow jams. Judas tripped on me the whole time, accusing me of being in love already. I fronted and called it relaxing, but he knew something was wrong when I turned down his proposal to sneak out of our dorm after curfew and go to a strip club. Normally I would've beaten him out of the hotel, but now my mind was preoccupied. We lost the game, but that didn't matter. All I could see was Monday.

Monday came, but I didn't hear from Teresa to see what time we were gonna hook up. I waited, but there was no word. I finally called her and she was in her room. We talked casually for a moment and finally I asked her if we were supposed to hook up. She said yes, but that she had an accounting test the next day and that it wasn't a good night. I got irritated and asked her why she hadn't called me, mentioning that I thought it was inconsiderate and that I had better things to do than sit around and wait for her (that was really smart, Ken!). She replied that she didn't ask me to wait on her. I'd made that choice. Her schoolwork was the most important thing right now. I told her that I wasn't trying to interfere with her schoolwork, and that she apparently didn't have time for someone in her life. She said that I was probably right. I was mad and hung up the phone without saying goodbye.

Though I was angry, I was more disappointed. How could I let my emotions take over like that? I should've tried to reschedule, but all I could see was instant gratification. To my surprise, two weeks later I got a call. I was thrilled when I heard Teresa's voice. We both apologized and confessed to over-reacting. She asked for a rain check and I gladly obliged. Not long after that, she became my girl. We would go to the park and spend hours talking with each other. It was like heaven. The only problem was that I already had a girl at home.

I was deceiving both of them and, regardless of my lusts, I knew that wasn't right. How could I let my relationship with Teresa continue on a foundation of deception? I knew how she felt about guys that talked to her when they had girlfriends. Her last boyfriend did that and she broke up with him as soon as she found out. She broke up with Juan when she saw him holding hands with Vera. Because of that, I felt as if I couldn't risk telling her, after all that we went through.

My reasons for breaking up with Michelle had very little to do with Teresa. We'd been heading that way prior to dating Teresa. A couple of months later, Michelle and I talked face to face and agreed to go our separate ways.

Life is nothing if not ironic. As time passed, I began to realize that Teresa and I were growing apart and something was missing in our relationship. I graduated from A&T, and Teresa was finishing her last year at Bennett. This seemed to open a rift between us. We were headed in different directions fast. We discussed marriage, but I wasn't ready for a commitment. Teresa left. It was for the best, but that didn't make it any easier. I learned that even if you love something, the time may come where you have to let go. Each person that comes into your life plays a role and helps to shape the future.

I was hurting and found a lot of comfort in my friend Simona. She was the only close female friend that I had during this period. I'd met her during my college years. She'd dated one of the players on the football team. I'd always had a schoolboy crush on her, but between her dating one of my teammates and me dating Teresa, nothing had ever developed. By now I had become so close to her that it would be like dating my sister. Granted, while Teresa and I were having problems, there was a peaked curiosity, but I wouldn't allow myself to entertain it seriously. Simona was able to help me work through some of my feelings about Teresa. She also taught me a lot about different types of relationships, and how they can also mold your life.

One night I was hanging out with some friends at Simona's house and her friend Karen came over. I'll admit, I thought she was cute when I first saw her. She had pretty eyes and beautiful skin. Though she was heavyset, her weight didn't take away from her looks. I spent most of that night telling stupid jokes and making faces. I wasn't really concerned about what she thought about me, because I wasn't trying to get with her. Initially, I thought she was stuck up, and of course that didn't impress me. She didn't smile much, and when she did, it looked fake. In all fairness, I'm sure I didn't make the greatest impression on her either.

We spent most of the night making small talk, with Simona interjecting periodically to make the conversation flow. Karen mentioned that she had a child. The night ended without either of us attempting to pursue the other. Still, Simona pressured me about her. I told her that I'd only talked to Karen as a favor to her. Regardless, for whatever reason, she felt strongly that Karen and I had made a connection.

I had no more contact with Karen until over a year later when I called Simona and she said that Karen was there. Before I had a chance to tell her that I didn't want to talk to her, she had put Karen on the phone. We chatted for a minute and I gave her my number, not expecting her to call (and not really caring either way). To my surprise she did call, and I must say we had some very interesting conversations. Eventually, I invited her over for a card game. Because I hadn't seen her in over a year, I didn't know what to expect. We ended up having a very enjoyable evening.

Over time I found myself wanting to be around her. I thought I was innocent because I wasn't looking for a relationship and she had just had a baby. Most of the time, things like relationships show up and you don't even know what's happened. As time passed I began to feel comfortable telling her my dreams. She was the first woman who ever got excited about my plans, which was weird because I didn't want anyone getting close to me. Karen and I were just friends. I tried not to think anything more of it, but over time our friendship grew deeper and deeper. It eventually led us to marriage. Friendship is the cornerstone to any relationship. It allows you to care about the person and learn about what makes them tick without passing judgement or being selfish.

I thought the true meaning of being a man was to love as many women as possible, but learned the truth once I met Karen. The measure of a man is to love one woman a whole lifetime.

Whosoever findeth a wife, findeth a good thing, and obtaineth favor of the Lord. – Proverbs 18:22

Many times I had heard this piece of scripture since giving my life to God, but didn't fully understand the meaning until I was able to understand the idea of loving a women a whole lifetime. Karen came into my life and taught me one of the most valuable lessons of life: unconditional love. In hindsight, my previous relationships were based solely on feelings. There was no depth. If things were going well on a daily basis, the relationship must be good. Unconditional love is based on a commitment that bonds your soul to another person during the tough times. God wanted to show man what he was like through the goodness of a woman.

A Good Woman.....

A Good woman loves you through the arguments, disagreements, and disappointments - so does God

A good woman supports you through your mistakes and failures - so does God

A good woman wants you to be more than you have become - so does God

A good woman is your strength when you're weak - so is God

A good woman soothes your pain when you're hurting - so does God

A good woman wants you to grow to your maximum potential - so does God

A good woman wants you to sow seeds to help others - so does God

All of the answers to my questions, all the missing pieces in my life were all found in Karen. Our relationship rounded out my life, making me a whole person. Each faltered relationship in the past

God, I ain't trying to hear all that!

prepared me for my best friend and lover who I love unconditionally.

God, I ain't trying to hear all that!

God, I ain't trying to hear all that!

CHAPTER FIVE:

We All Need A Dream

After I graduated from college I was left with an empty feeling inside. Although I had spent five years in school and had helped to take a football team from losing to winning its first conference championship, I was still lacking a sense of accomplishment. Here I was with a college degree, yet I was living on the floor of a friend's apartment, working a temporary job at a local mill. I felt as though my life had little or no direction. The "real world" was a scary place. Companies were out to make a profit and employees were the workhorses who were going to make it happen. Going to a predominantly black school, I had been sheltered from a racist society. I thought it was a thing of the past.

Working at the mill opened my eyes to a whole new world. I had been raised to speak to everyone, and be courteous. Look people in the eyes and greet them with a smile. At the mill most of the white people went out of their way to try and avoid eye contact. They hardly spoke to me or to any of the other black people. I began to boil inside, wondering if this was how the rest of my life would be.

I eventually left the mill and took a job with one of the world's largest companies as a security guard. The pay was better so I decided it was time to find my own place and get my life on track. The situation there was much better. Blacks and whites communicated frequently. I didn't get the feeling of segregation, but I experienced something different that was just as bothersome: Classism—the separation of the "have's" and "have-not's". I was a have-not. Upper management treated the rest of us as mere slaves of the system. It appeared our opinions and ideas meant nothing. The color of the playing field was neither black nor white; it was green. The company only cared about one thing: making money. I felt the same anger and resentment I had experienced at the mill. This anger, combined with the lack of accomplishment I felt, made me boil. I decided I was going to do something for myself. I was going to take control of my life and determine my own destiny. I was ready to get to the next level and find that greater purpose.

My mother always told me to make my request known to God and he'll hear me. I remember sitting in a half-furnished dirty apartment, no money in my pocket, asking God to help me find my purpose and give me the strength and stamina to make my dreams become a reality. I began reading everything I could get my hands on about successful people and their struggles in making it to the top of the game. I learned that successful people have two things in common: a clear vision and the passion to see that vision become a reality.

The more I read the more excited and enthusiastic I became. I realized my prayers had been answered. I was beginning to plant the seeds for my future success. Each morning I woke up with purpose and direction. I had decided to start my own business and live the American dream.

It's amazing what happens when you ask God for help and receive a revelation. Life was immediately different for me. I felt different inside. The anger disappeared and was replaced by enthusiasm. In times past, my motive for going into business was strictly to make a profit so that I could live the good life with nice clothes, cars, and plenty of money. I wanted to look good in the eyes of others, but the more I studied the Word of God, the more of a passion I had to go into business to *help* others.

I heard my pastor say on numerous occasions, "What you make happen for others, God will make happen for you." I took this to heart. I became hungry for the Word of God, and as I studied, I saw how much the Bible talked about money, wealth, and prosperity. I wondered why so many Christians were barely making it from paycheck to paycheck. Three scriptures that I always took to heart were 2 Corinthians 9:8, Isaiah 1:19, and Psalm 1:3. Each of these tells us that God desires his people to be wealthy and have more than enough.

More and more I began to see people in the church that often talked of big things, but never did anything with their ideas. The more I studied, the more motivated I became. For me it was a no-brainer; I had to go into the entrepreneurial field. It seemed like every idea, every concept, every opportunity was calling me, whether I heard them from other people or I read them in a magazine. My friend, Page, was working in the computer business at the time, but shared my passion and ideas. We both wanted to help others and reach our pot of gold. I was frequently calling him to see if he was going to be coming to Greensboro so that we could go into business together.

Page finally came back to Greensboro in 1990. He had already started a business called "Ident-I-Kid", where he would go into the school system and make identification badges for the kids. They were actually for the parents in case the child turned up missing. It was easy for him to bring the business to North Carolina because there were no restrictions. In the meantime, I started a balloon wrapping business. A machine would blow up the balloons while stretching them enough that they could be filled with all sorts of gifts, including jewelry, teddy bears, clothes, etc. The balloons would then be wrapped as a gift.

While others were getting things wrapped, I was looking for the number to the company that made the machine. When I called them, they told me I needed about $2,500 to get started. At the time, I was only making about $5.00 per hour and $2,500 seemed like quite a bit. I decided to talk to a guy named Frank McCain. Frank was very vocal in the student government when we were in school and, though I didn't know him very well, I took my chances. He came through for us, and the loan was approved. With that, I was on my way.

I was dreaming and thinking bigger than I had ever before. Carl Sandberg once said, "nothing happens that isn't first a dream." Dreaming is essential to destiny and having God's best in your life. No dream is impossible to achieve with God on your side. Dreaming is one of the most powerful abilities that God has given us. It is God's way of allowing us to see ourselves the way He sees us.

Be Careful What You Wish For

With Page back in Greensboro, our team was finally formed. We had two businesses that we were running, the balloon business on holidays and the Indent-I-Kid business on a regular basis. However, we found ourselves facing some obstacles. For the balloon business, Valentine's Day and Christmas were our two biggest periods. We made great money during those seasons, but were forced to put in a lot of very long hours. Because the Ident-I-Kid headquarters placed limitations to which counties you could be in, and because someone was already stationed in Greensboro, we had to drive thirty miles to Winston-Salem. We couldn't afford to pay anyone to do the badges, so we worked extremely hard to get the job done, sometimes staying up until 1:00 a.m. finishing badges that were due the next day. Between the two companies, we had more work than we could manage. During the busy season, we often worked 14-hour days. Though we were motivated by the potential profit, our profit was barely enough to pay us a small salary after considering our cost of goods sold. The glamour of owning our own business faded quickly.

The first lesson I ever learned in business was that it didn't matter how hard you worked, the trick was learning to work smart. I knew that building a successful business was a process, but I didn't expect that you had to kill yourself. There were days that we would drive all the way to Winston to deliver two or three I.D. badges. We knew that there had to be a better way to provide quality customer service and still be efficient.

At this time, Page approached me about bringing on some help. He already had someone in mind: a friend from school named Phil White. I was reluctant initially for two reasons. First, he hadn't sacrificed what we had sacrificed. Second, Page was talking of giving him partial ownership even though Phil was not going to be putting money into the company. He had lost his job selling insurance, and now he wanted to go into business.

Even though we had played football together, I wasn't sure if Phil was the right person to go into business with. Did he have that killer instinct? However, I knew that he was a nice, mild-mannered guy that was easy to like. He had always been able to control his temper and that was an asset. After considering all of the possibilities, we decided mutually that his assets outweighed his potential liabilities and he joined the team. The only thing that frightened me was that we were all friends with big dreams. I had heard countless stories of friends that didn't make good business partners.

Meanwhile, I was looking for something more. I mean, I was grateful for what God had blessed us with, but I wanted more. I wanted something that wouldn't be limited to my geographical region. I had once heard someone say that if you sell to the classes, you'll live with the masses, but if you sell to the masses, you'll live with the classes. In other words, we needed something that could touch a lot of people. I went back to God in prayer. I prayed that God would give me a vision of something bigger than us.

Page had, on occasion, told us about a vision he had of owning a large advertising agency. Now, that idea seemed to be the answer we were looking for. We formed an entity called Tel-Ad Marketing Services. The concept was simple. The company would sell you a wooden display. You would then place the display in hotels, convention centers, airports, etc.; anywhere tourists or visitors might be. The displays were free to the hotels and other displaying areas, funded by advertising. The hotel wanted them in the lobby because they were convenient for guests.

Upon placing the display, you would then sell advertising space to businesses. There was a phone line listed on the display, which allowed interested customers to contact the respective business just by pressing a button. Though this sounded good in theory, the application was much harder. First, you had to find places to put the signs. After that, you had to convince people to call.

We had two placed, one at the Airport Marriott, the other at the Chamber of Commerce. Page really believed in the idea and because I believed in him, I gave it my all. Eventually, I sold more ads than Page or Phil; not that it was a competition, I just believe that anything you do should be done to the fullest. Something burned inside of me. Even though I gave my all to this, I felt unfulfilled. I couldn't see myself doing this for a long period of time. In the midst of all this, we were still doing our I.D. badges. Because we were splitting our time and energy between two businesses, both businesses suffered.

A few months later, we noticed that nothing was working. We were broke. I started working at a group home just to survive, but all of that money was going to the expansion of the business. Nobody was getting paid because we had no money. Ident-I-Kid was becoming a burden. The cost and time to do the business was killing us. We had scaled our efforts from trying to get large elementary and middle schools, to trying to get daycare centers with twenty students or less. Sometimes, we would have to take the money made just to get gas to return home. If we decided to eat, that was even less money. We never expected to have to work so hard just to get gas and eat lunch.

God, I ain't trying to hear all that!

Though we didn't have much money, our spirits were never broken. We knew that tomorrow would be a brighter day. The Bible teaches in Proverbs that a wise man is open to new ideas, in fact, he looks for them. I was always looking for new ideas and concepts. I turned to God again, and began to pray for more insight into my future. My prayers would be answered once again. Every step we take in our journey prepares us for the next adventure. Even though we weren't getting the results we desired from our current business endeavors, they served a great purpose. God wanted us to experience difficult situations and circumstances so that we would be prepared when success came. Dreams are what keep you going through the tough times. Our dreams sustained us through ours.

God, I ain't trying to hear all that!

God, I ain't trying to hear all that!

CHAPTER SIX

Persistence Prevails

My mother has always told me to pray when you need answers, and that God will give them to you. As I faced a point in my life where I was uncertain of which direction to go in, I turned to that advice. As I prayed, images of success began to overwhelm me. Visions of helping others attain success kept going through my head. The words "if you sell to the classes you will live with the masses, but if you sell to the masses, you'll live with the classes" kept running through my mind like a broken record.

I was sitting at the end of my bed the next morning reading Entrepreneur Magazine. I read an article about a guy that had received permission to use famous paintings and put those images on watches. The article instantly caught my attention. As I read more, this individual even put pictures of famous people like Dan Quayle on watch faces, and sold hundreds of them. A light bulb flipped on. Why not put black art onto watches? This would appeal to a large segment of the population not previously targeted. Shows like The Cosby Show were booming, and my partners and I decided this would be our next business venture. We were going to rekindle the appreciation of black art. I was excited.

I asked God for help with this idea, and overnight I was provided with a vision. As I began to think more and more about the ideas for this venture, it dawned on me that my parents had recently bought a new home and were filling it with collections of fine black art from a local art dealer. I decided to make a trip home and go talk to the woman who was the dealer to see what I could find out about the artists or if she could assist me in contacting them.

I walked into the store feeling nervous. I wasn't sure what I was going to say, so I walked around pretending to be looking. A lady came up to me and asked if I needed any help.

"How do I get in touch with some of the artists that created these wonderful paintings in your store?" I asked.

She slid her reading glasses down onto her narrow nose, and aimed her eyes out over the rim at me. I saw suspicion in them.

"Do you sell art?"

"No," I replied, "but I am looking to get some done."

She interrogated me for about ten minutes, asking all types of questions but never revealing her source. A major roadblock, but I had the courage to overcome it. I knew that if I was going to make this watch thing become a reality I was going to have to first find a way to get to these artists, and then find a company that could print full color photos on watch faces. Not to mention that fact that I was going to need money, and lots of it.

I started at the most obvious place: the library. I looked in the Thomas Registry for all the watch manufactures in the United States. I started calling vendor after vendor, but no one could do what I needed done and no one had a clue where to go. I knew the technology was out there, I just had to find it. I was spending countless hours gathering information, making phone calls and asking questions just trying to get some answers. My persistence paid off when I found a company that not only could do what I wanted, but seemed just as excited about the idea as me. The manufacturer was confident he could do a great job and offered to print a sample watch for us. We were delighted to say the least.

We sent a photo and patiently sat and waited for the sample. The anticipation was worse than waiting to open presents on Christmas morning. We were on our way and everyone was excited. The creative juices started flowing. Eric immediately came up with the idea to call our new venture BAG (black art gear). Finally, after four weeks we received the sample back. We were very pleased with how the watch looked, and felt confident that this manufacturer could get the job done. One obstacle down, two to go. Now we needed to find our artists and a way to scrape up some money.

God, I ain't trying to hear all that!

The Search is On

Money and resources are just minor obstacles if you have true passion for what you're doing. I immediately headed down to a local art gallery that had an exhibit to try and find more information. It just so happened they were displaying the black art of local unknown artists. This was perfect. Our best chance of striking a deal would be with one of them. They would be looking to get their name out.

I walked through the galleria, and two particular pieces kept staring back at me. One combined a space-aged robot with shackles from the slave era. The other piece depicted women along with two black men in shackles. These pieces stood out because of the colors and strong images. I asked the museum for the artists' names and phone numbers, and without hesitation they gave me everything I needed to know.

The next challenge was to try and sell the artists on the idea. My father always said the master salesman is the one who can close any deal with anyone when sitting with them face to face. I was up to the challenge.

I made contact and scheduled a meeting with the first artist who happened to be a graduate of A&T, which immediately gave us common ground. I thought that surely this must be our guy. He came to my office for the meeting, and the first thing that struck me was his arrogance and cockiness. I told him all about our idea and what we were trying to do, and he just sat there motionless with a blank stare on his face. Finally he spoke.

"I don't want my art to be belittled on some cheap watch faces that you're trying to push."

Just like that our meeting ended. I was disappointed, but instead of ending the dream right there I made the decision that no one was going to keep me from obtaining my vision.

I called the other artist and scheduled a meeting with him. Desperate to get this thing rolling, I insisted we meet the next day. He told me to come down to his apartment. When I arrived the next day, I was taken back by where he lived. His name was Eddie. He had small, beady eyes and wire framed glasses. We chatted for a while. He was a little more down to earth than his appearance first led me to believe. He explained to me his thoughts and the motives behind his creativity. After hearing how the picture of the two men and the women depicted our relationship between the sexes, he stressed his interest in our project and felt his art was worthy.

We started discussing money and I told him we would be offering an up front fee plus 10% of sales. He replied that his artwork was more than unique, and each painting was worth $400 plus 15% of sales. I tried to negotiate down, but this guy wouldn't budge.

Unsure of how I was going to pay him, and not knowing if we would ever sell a watch, I told him I would get back with him. So I left and continued my search for an artist, knowing that they weren't going to be easy to deal with. It just so happened that I met a woman who was enthusiastic about trying to help me. She ran the Greensboro Cultural Art Center and was more than willing to give me a name of a really good nationally known painter that lived in Greensboro. His name was Hallasie. He was a big-hearted guy that had a good reputation. I was nervous about meeting with him because one local artist had already knocked the project and another wanted more than we could afford to give. I was worried that this guy was going to laugh at me or be angry for wasting his time. I prayed the entire way over to see him, hoping this would be the defining moment.

I arrived at his house and was instantly attracted to the elegance of the place. I explained to him my dream of having fine black American art on the faces of watches and clocks. He listened intently, then asked, "why should I trust you?"

I wasn't prepared for that. I sat there gazing into his eyes and without conscious effort started telling him how I was struggling with my feelings. I told him that one night I had sat praying for guidance from God and the next morning I'd awakened with this vision. I told him that I was passionate about seeing this project happen. I started to say more and he stopped me.

"I listened to you," he said, "now I want you to listen to me. I believe you have a good idea, but I have seen many entrepreneurs with good intentions go awry, leaving the artist holding the short end of the stick. Usually by providing their work and never getting paid." There was a long pause where time seemed to stand still, then he continued. "I believe you. I want $1,500 up front and 30% of the profits." Inside I was thinking there was no way. I told him I would love to pay him that, but my partners and I didn't have that kind of money. He responded by telling me he would settle for 15%, and that we could work out an arrangement for the up front money. I could tell that this artist was more concerned about his art than about money. His integrity impressed me.

In just a short time we had made part of this dream become a reality. Pieces of the puzzle were starting to fit together and we were getting more and more excited. With two artists committed, I knew we needed to get one more just to be safe and to have variety. There was a print called Black is Black by a painter who went under the name Poncho. He had one of the hottest prints out at the time and we knew we needed to get his permission to use it as our signature piece. I called and left a message for him several times over the course of two weeks. Finally I called and asked his secretary if he'd received my messages. We'd built something of a rapport from my prior phone calls.

"You sure are persistent, aren't you?" she asked. "What is it that you want from him?"

I told her about my vision and how his work would be the perfect match for our project. She explained that he received hundreds of calls like this, and because of bad experiences in the past he really was not open to new ideas.

God, I ain't trying to hear all that!

"But," she said, "you seem adamant about this. Call back at two and I'll send you through to him."

Fair enough. Two o'clock rolled around and I made the call. Both nervous and excited, I introduced myself and started to tell him how much I liked his work. He stopped me and said, "What is it that you want?" I reluctantly started to tell him about the vision and he immediately said, "No, not at all interested."

"Wait, please. I will drive six hours to your office in Baltimore if you will give me just fifteen minutes of your time. Would you be willing to do that?"

It was quiet, then he answered. "Sure."

Eric and I drove the six hours to get there. We were both very nervous. I knew that if we sat face-to-face, there would be no way he could turn us down. My father had always said, "People don't believe in ideas, they believe in you and your ability to make the idea a reality." This must have been true, because our fifteen-minute meeting turned into a two-hour discussion ultimately leading to an agreement. Finally, after numerous rejections and a lack of help, we managed to get three artists, two nationally known. We had the first piece of the puzzle completed, now we had to turn our attention to the hardest part: getting the money to fund our venture.

Eric, Phil and I wrote out a business plan. It was shot down by several banks and investors. In a last ditch effort we decided to go to Wachovia bank and pitch the idea in hopes of receiving $100,000, which would be enough to get us started. We had the manufacturer, we had the artists; we just needed the money. We put the plan together and pitched it to a banker named Mike who seemed excited about the idea. He took it to the committee who had the final say. They rejected it.

Meanwhile, Phil had been doing his homework and found a trade show called the MAGIC SHOW, where thousands of retailers come to see new wares from manufacturers. Problem was that it was going to cost us $8,500 to attend the show. Plus, we had only two low quality samples and no money, but where there's a dream, there's a way. We started asking our friends and family members for money. We didn't care about the samples, we just knew we needed to be at this show. We were willing to walk if need be. We were going to be there. Our persistence paid off and we managed to borrow enough to make our way to Las Vegas, Nevada. Though we managed to jump this hurdle, we were faced with yet another dilemma: we only had two watches for display. In desperation, Eric came up with a plan. We would buy some cheap watches, disassemble them and place our artwork on the dial. Not having any other options, the night before the show, we sat up into the wee hours getting these display watches ready so that we could show off our idea the next morning. We knew if we could just give people a glimpse of our idea, we would be able to sell them and then figure out how we were going to get them made.

God, I ain't trying to hear all that!

Our persistence and determination paid off again. After working the show for three days, we managed to get $10,000 in orders and caught the attention of a marketing consultant that had contacts with QVC and the Home Shopping Network, along with major retail stores. She liked our idea and felt she could help us get our product out to the masses. With $10,000 in orders, some good contacts and a strong sense of accomplishment, all three of us sat on the plane headed home with smiles on our face. We knew we had taken an idea and turned it into a reality, despite having been faced with numerous obstacles, a lack of money and no guidance.

There is always a way to reach your goal. You have to have that inner drive and determination to go out and get it. Persistence is key. Many times we think a plan has to go a certain way, and if it doesn't we abandon our dream and chalk it up as a bad idea. Sometimes success is just behind a closed door, and you have to kick it in to get it.

God, I ain't trying to hear all that!

CHAPTER SEVEN

Greed

We were excited when we got back from Vegas because we had received over $10,000 in orders and multiple contracts that would result in thousands of orders in the future. Our only problem was that we didn't have enough money to fill the orders we had gotten at the show. Still, we felt we had our bases covered; we could use the orders as leverage to work with Mike at the bank in getting a loan. When we returned, I called Mike to set up an appointment. He was anxious to meet with us and hear how things went in Vegas.

When we sat down to talk, he couldn't help but notice the smiles on our faces. We pulled the orders out and threw them on his desk, hoping it would sway him and the board to approve our loan. We told him about our meeting Eileen Stern in Vegas and her credentials. He asked if we'd give him her phone number.

Mike was the first person outside of our friends and family that believed in us. In spite of that, we had to continue to press because the bank loan was far from guaranteed. We had written a $2,500 hot check for the show display and owed money to friends and family. We were desperate and needed the loan in a bad way.

Pressing Toward the Mark

Our eyes remained fixed on our goals, which despite the aforementioned setbacks seemed to be getting closer and closer. Still, I honestly felt that the rest of the group believed in Eileen's story more than I did. She had spoken of having our products in stores across the country. It seemed too good to be true. Eileen told us to give her three weeks and she and her partner, Leslie Frank would meet us in Chicago to discuss their suggestions for our product line. About four weeks later, they called and told us to meet them in Chicago.

She greeted us warmly and was very personable. Their presentation was complete and impressive. They had obviously given our company and our product a great deal of thought. Their presentation included everything from product packaging and product displays, to point of purchase signs and future suggestions for increasing business. They had even outlined a plan to approach the large retailers that they were affiliated with. By the time we left, we were in awe. Now more than ever, I was convinced that we had a winning product and couldn't wait to show it to the world.

Family Affair

About a week and a half after we returned from Chicago, Mike Wilkerson from the bank, called and told us that he had finally gotten the board and the Small Business Administration to approve our loan. I was about to bust, and my happiness seeped through the phone. All I could think was, thank you Jesus! First the meeting with Eileen went well, and now this. It was the perfect day and I couldn't think of what could go wrong, but the day changed in a couple of seconds. No sooner had he told us that the loan was approved, he added that the bank would finance 70% of the loan. That rocked our world. Though he spoke of it nonchalantly, it was a major concern for us. I asked him what he meant when he said the bank would only finance 70% of the loan. Simply put, he said that the bank was going to give us $70,000 of the $100,000 that we needed to get started. He said that this was a typical deal because the bank usually wanted the business to put about 30% of the money needed into the deal, so as to assume some of the risk. Therefore, if the deal went bad, the bank wasn't the only one to lose. The owner would have a vested interest in the project and be more motivated to see it succeed. After the math, we needed to come up with about $25,000, when we could barely come up with $25.

By this time, my dad was thoroughly convinced about the business. It really didn't surprise me when he offered to help us. Now my father wasn't a wealthy man, nor did he have $25,000 lying around, but he believed in paying bills on time and protecting his credit. He made a comfortable living for himself and my mother. When I explained to him our situation, he thought over all of the specifics of the deal, then said that he would call us back in two days. When the two days had passed, he called and told me how much he and my mother believed in me and the business that we were working. They decided to take out a home equity loan for the $25,000 that we needed to close the deal. I knew that it was a huge sacrifice, especially since my mother had suffered a stroke the year before, paralyzing her on the left side and leaving her unable to work. In addition to that, the insurance company had denied some of the claims and had stuck my dad with some of the medical bills. Regardless, he still insisted on helping us. It meant the world to me that they believed in me that much. I was apprehensive with my excitement because, while I wanted to take the money, I didn't want my parents to risk losing their home.

Time for Success

Two roads that are paved with good intentions are the road to hell and the road to failure. Good intentions simply want to get the job done, but are unwilling to do the extras that it takes to be truly successful. From the day we signed the deal with the bank, I felt a sense of desperation. I understood that success was predicated on focusing and achieving your goals and that obstacles only took over when you lost focus, but they were a part of business and life.

Initially, things started slow. We ran into problems, especially with the shipment of our watches from Hong Kong, because of customs. When we finally did get the watches, we had problems with them from the printing on our watches being either too light or too dark. Our Hong Kong manufacturer wasted hundreds of watch dials because they were printed too close together. Then we dealt with a lack of response when we did our first mail order campaign. I thought people would see our brochure and just begin ordering. Out of 1,000 mail-outs, we got about ten orders.

Page and I had been arguing about whether or not to sell wholesale. He felt we would make money because of volume and profit margin if we allowed retailers to distribute the product to its customers. On the other hand, I felt we could have a successful mail order operation based on the success that we had with our friends and family members. It was ridiculous for me to assume that because those close to us bought our watches like hot cakes, others would as well. I learned that I didn't know as much as I thought I did concerning the mail order industry. I had to constantly perfect my marketing tactics. Because we had to win at any cost, my approach was pragmatic. We went back to the drawing board to prove ourselves worthy of the success that we so desperately desired. Initially, we had a tough time and it wasn't fun because there was so much more at stake.

After about six months in the business we were barely making it and we needed a break. Fortunately, some things began to go right for us. Slowly but surely, the word was getting around about our product line. Most of our customers were small retailers with specialty or art stores. We appreciated them because they believed in our product enough to buy it and they appreciated us because we were easy to work with and down to earth.

One day Leslie Frank called and said that she had spoken with a representative from QVC about our product and they wanted to meet us. Because we had done the things that she suggested we do, we were ready for the opportunity. Phil and I went to New York to meet with the QVC representative. It was apparent throughout the meeting that the woman liked our watches, and after the presentation she wasted no time in giving us a chance. She said that her initial order would be 1,800 watches. Phil was never one to show his emotions, but I was about to burst. So many things were going through my mind, including the profit we would make.

We sealed the deal, the date was set. Leslie and Eileen asked me to go on the show and sell the watches. Though I was nervous, I agreed. Besides I had three months to prepare; it was November and we were going on in February for Black History Month (go figure!).

Sky's the Limit

Things were happening for us now at a monster pace. Around the same time we had gone to visit QVC, we had been introduced to the buyer from the Home Shopping Network. They had recently formed an alliance with BET called BET Shop, where the Home Shopping Network would provide its services including order taking and shipping. BET provided the major network and geared all products to the black community. I thought it was a perfect fit. Their initial order was for 600 watches, with 200 of them being a commemorative that we did because of the movie "Tuskegee Airmen." Though we had just finished the sample and didn't even have it with us, the buyer wanted it because it was an exclusive and she loved notoriety.

We were finally beginning to see the fruits of our labor. People believed in our product. We agreed that we would air the Tuskegee watch on BET Shop, because of the movie release date and the hype that had been created. BET Shop was our big test to see how a broad market would respond to us. That October day I had butterflies in my stomach. The show lasted only two hours. Six o'clock came and went, then six-thirty, and I began to get nervous. But at exactly 6:41, I saw the announcement of the commemorative watch. Within four minutes the watches sold out. I couldn't believe it. We had sold 200 watches in four minutes! Two weeks later, we had two more watches on the show, and this time the buyer invited us to be on the show. We decided that Phil would go since I was going to be on QVC. It took six minutes this time, but we sold out of all of our watches once again. By then, BET Shop was sure of the validity of our business and our product.

Palmer and I flew to the QVC headquarters in West Chester, which is just a few miles outside of Philadelphia. We were a huge success, selling over 1,000 watches in less than 20 minutes. Calls were coming in from all over the country from whites and blacks to talk with me about our product. The results from this publicity were astounding. We began getting free publicity from various sources. Essence Magazine, The Source Magazine, and Black Enterprise, all did feature articles on our company and our products. Our local newspaper, The Greensboro News and Record did a full-page feature on us.

Steady Moving

Business continued to boom, and one day we got a call from CNN requesting a representative of our company to come and be on one of their live shows to talk about the product. By this time we had agreed to hire Alan Palmer full time as a sales manager, capitalizing on his business savvy to help take us to the next level. For the CNN interview, Palmer went with me. Again, people loved our product. Eventually we were getting orders from

Spiegel Catalog, Target Stores, Sears, and Army Air Force Exchange. Our product had been on the Shopping Network seven different times. With all of our response came a growing market for people looking for custom watches, so much so that we began to accommodate their request. Essence Magazine, The Nation of Islam, Martin Luther King Jr. Center, and the Bishop Man Ministries were some of our biggest customers for custom watches. Life was good, but there was always more money to make. I can remember looking at bank statements when our account had over $100,000 in it. Though I knew it wasn't all ours, seeing it in our account sent a chill up my spine. It felt good to have control of that much money.

The Root of Evil

Growing up I heard that money was the root of all evil. As I got older the scripture rang true, although in my opinion it was actually the **love** of money that was the root of all evil. Being broke causes you to see that from a different perspective; a lack of money can cause you to do some evil things. People are motivated to rob, kill, and commit other criminal acts when they have nothing. Now that we had access to money, I understood both sides of the fence. On the flip side, when there is a large amount of money involved, there is the potential for greed to creep in and ruin a good thing.

Money can give you a false sense of security, because you feel like your money can solve any problem that you have. Money made me

God, I ain't trying to hear all that!

arrogant and overconfident, and that began to cost me in life and business. Eventually, I started buying things that I probably could have done without. The first thing I did was lease a new car, a 1996 Volvo 850. My suits could no longer be purchased off the rack, I had to have them custom made and I wore them with an air of confidence. When people think that you have money or status they treat you differently. For the next year and a half, we were on an upward swing and it seemed like we couldn't be stopped. Our accounts continued to flourish and new business continued to pour in. I couldn't think of anything that could possibly go wrong. Little did I know that what was around the corner would make me temporarily forget all of the success that we were having.

My personal goal was to grow the company to a million dollars. Because of our current run of success, we felt we could get a contract from nearly any company. Our merchandise was in high demand and we were getting requests for custom / theme watches. One day when I walked into Phil's house, he and Palmer were watching a television evangelist, the Bishop Man . I commented on the vibrant colors of his suits. Because he was a big man, colorful and bright suits stood out on him a bit more than the average person. Phil suggested that we try to contact him about possibly doing some work with him for one of his conferences.

God, I ain't trying to hear all that!

Get Ready! Get Ready! Get Ready . . . for Trouble!

Phil educated me on a couple of things regarding the Bishop Man's ministry. First, he let me know that he had a following that was increasing by leaps and bounds. Second, he told me about the two major conferences that he held annually: "Men of God" and "Women of God!" Each conference was geared toward the particular gender, advertised and served as a time of inspiration, healing, and reconciliation back to God. We were particularly interested in The Men's Conference. Men would come from all over the country to worship and get encouragement on being better fathers, husbands, and men overall. Phil showed me a tape of the previous year's conference and I was totally taken aback. I was amazed at all of the men, particularly black men that were there, loving each other and worshipping God. Seeing this event was great inspiration, both spiritually and from a business perspective.

The tape and Phil's suggestion caused a light bulb in my head to go off. Immediately, I began to think of different ways that we could pull it off. I knew that if we could, we would have a tremendous payday ahead of us. It was all about making more money.

Because we didn't know him, and his ministry was so large, I knew it would be almost impossible to get a conversation with him just by picking up the phone and calling his office. There had to be another way. Then it dawned on me. A member of our church named John Gatling, reportedly sold custom-made suits to the Bishop Man, but I wasn't sure if it was true or not.

One day, I saw John at UPS picking up a package and decided I would break the ice. I spoke with enthusiasm, asking him how he had been. I found out that John was a lot like me, ambitious and driven to be successful. We talked of our business endeavors and our roads traveled in getting to Christ, and by the end of the conversation we had built a kinship. While discussing his business, he told me how he'd gotten to meet the Bishop Man. A friend of his, a pastor, had introduced them. He gave me the pastor's number. John called him first to vouch for me. The pastor was excited about meeting me and we set an appointment to meet in my office.

Before he arrived, I laid out all of the products we had done in the past in the conference room. He arrived with his son, and when they saw the products their faces lit up. His son loved our tee shirts, and said he knew lots of students that would wear them once they hit the market. I could tell the pastor was buying our concept. I explained to him that I wanted to do custom products for the Men and Women of God conferences, with artwork designed to represent all ethnic backgrounds. Designs would be placed on watches, bags, shirts, etc. and could be used as a reminder of the conference experience after the participants left. I could see the excitement on his face. I instructed him that when he called not to try to sell the concept, just get the meeting set up. If I got the meeting, I assumed the rest would be history. He said that he would get back with me in a couple of weeks and let me know what happened. Though he would try his best and use his influence, he couldn't promise anything.

Less than a week later he called and wanted to know if I could leave for Dallas the next Friday. He said that he had been invited to a pastor's conference that the Bishop Man was having, and that prior to the service that night there would be a Men of God committee meeting. When I asked him if he'd talked with the Bishop Man about meeting with me, he told me not to worry about it and guaranteed that I would get to meet with him.

The pastor had one of his assistants fly with me and by the time we arrived in Dallas, he was already there and had arranged for someone to pick us up. As we arrived at the Bishop's church, perched atop a hill, I was amazed at the size, structure, and beauty. It seated 5,000 people. In spite of the many churches I had been to, I had never seen one of this magnitude. When we got to the front entrance, we were immediately directed to a meeting room upstairs. This was the meeting of the Men of God Committee. They planned the events and made decisions concerning the conference. When I went in I was welcomed as a friend of the pastor's. It was like a who's who of pastors and preachers. I could remember seeing several of them on television. I thought to myself, Wow! Here I was standing in the midst of these men of God, all of whom I respected.

Finally, after a couple of hours, we met the Bishop Man in the main sanctuary. The pastor told him that I was the guy he'd told him about with the good idea. The Bishop Man asked me my name, thanked me for coming and assured me that we would sit and talk. His office was directly behind the pulpit where he preached. As we approached the entrance it got dark. We were lead up a narrow staircase towards a door at the top. The pastor gave me a signal and I began to explain my idea. Though the Bishop didn't seem overly enthused, he did hear me out. I thought of him as a pastor, but also as a businessman and tailored my presentation as such. I told him about the thought of merchandising his conference, that we could make products that flow with the theme of the conference, and that our artists could custom design artwork for the merchandise. When he began to see the potential, his eyes lit up. Sure, they had sold tee shirts in the past, but they had never had merchandising at the magnitude of what I was proposing.

After I had run my sales pitch, he looked at me firmly and asked me about the money arrangement. That was something that I had been contemplating in my mind the entire trip. I thought about making him a partner in the venture, meaning that we both put in money and split the profit, but then there would really be no benefit for him in the deal. My other thought was that we handle everything, from up front cost, manufacturing, and merchandising, to shipping, set up, etc. This seemed the most viable because the ministry had very little responsibility and we assumed all the risk. Regardless, I was willing to take it because at the rate the ministry was growing, the potential greatly outweighed the risk. The second idea is what I approached him with. The whole time, I was trying to decide what percentage of gross sales I should give him. This meant they collected their money first, even before expenses were paid.

I decided that 10% of gross sales would be fair considering the ministry had nothing to lose. When I presented the figure to him, he laughed, and in his deep baritone voice said that Jesus got 10%, but not him. I was shocked and disappointed by the statement, not because he rejected my offer, but because of the allusions the statement drew. I then understood that I was no longer dealing with a pastor, but a businessman. The Bishop Man told me that he would get me in contact with Sam. Sam was his right hand man and handled all of the business endeavors of the church. Nothing was agreed to without his approval.

Sam had been with the Bishop Man since the beginning of the ministry, when the church was a storefront in West Virginia. As my meeting with the Bishop closed, he gave me Sam's number and told me that if Sam said it was okay, then the deal would be done. I knew then that I had to sell Sam on my concept without any help from another influential factor. When I finally got in touch with him, his demeanor was warm and friendly, that is until we started talking business. His warmth disappeared and he seemed to listen intently to what I was saying. After I finished he paused for a moment, then told me that the ministry had done it's own T-shirts for the Men's and Women of God conferences, and that they weren't interested in letting someone else do them.

When I felt the sale slipping away, I went into an all out sales blitz. There was no way I was going to let him tell me no and just take it. I knew the amount of money that was on the line and was willing to do anything to see this deal through. I mailed him samples, and after careful consideration he finally agreed to try us out at the "Women of God" conference scheduled for September 1996. If things went well he would strongly consider letting us do The Men's Conference on the East Coast in October.

When I talked with the Bishop he said that he was expecting 50,000 women, but Sam said that a more realistic number was between 30,000 and 35,000. The conference was scheduled for New Orleans in the Superdome. Regardless of whether there were 50,000 or 30,000, I was jumping for joy on the inside. This was our big break, and all of our hard work was about to pay off. I saw this as the tip of the iceberg, considering that there were numerous other conferences coming up. I was so excited about the potential that I left without all the details, and without talking through some of the key elements of our agreement. I figured working with men of God, I could trust that the details would work themselves out for everyone's good. My ignorance and greed would become the pitfall of our success. We were willing to accept any deal if it had the potential to make us money.

All I could think about was the money, and that we would be doing both conferences. I explained to Sam that we were putting up all the money for the products and would be responsible for shipping it to the Superdome. Again, I made my offer of 10% of gross revenues, still feeling confident that this was a fair deal considering the fact that we were taking all of the risk. His response caught me off guard. He told me that though we were taking all of the risk by manufacturing and shipping the product, it was the Bishop Man's Ministries that was creating the marketplace that would've otherwise been unavailable to us. Based on that, he felt as though the ministry deserved more money. Now, because of the Bishop's statement, I was already prepared to negotiate. The agreement was that we would do T-shirts, tote bags, and key chains for the conference. He felt the ministry should get 40% of the revenues on T-shirts and 30% on the key chains and tote bags. I was floored. I felt he was taking advantage of our desire to do this deal. I told him that the percentages were a bit high and his response to me was basically take it or leave it. Needless to say, when I got off the phone with Sam, I felt used, but I still saw this as an opportunity. If successful, we could potentially do all of their conferences, which would definitely be profitable for us in the long run.

The biggest dilemma that we were facing was how we were going to come up with the money so that we could get product for the 30,000 women that were expected. Our only hope was to seek out investors. My father already had a stake in our business. Although we didn't have a written contract with the ministry, we assumed a verbal agreement was solid enough because we were working with God's men. Having the verbal agreement in place, I talked with my partners about how we were going to raise the money. While we had a consistent stream of cash flow, we were still in debt, to the point that we were yet to be able to take a salary from the business.

If 30,000 women truly came, we could easily sell 10,000 T-shirts. We decided T-Shirts would sell for $15, tote bags would go for $10, and key chains would go for $2. We looked at the situation and saw that we had at least four things going for us. First, we were the only merchandise vendor at the conference. Second, the conference was only once a year, so people had to get it then or they wouldn't get it. Third, the ministry was backing us, which provided instant credibility and easy sales. And fourth, with over 30,000 people coming, if we sold to only a fraction of them we'd still sell out. We felt these points were strong enough to do the deal, though we knew that they were getting a lion's share. We'd been in business together a few years and felt like we knew how to analyze a deal. In actuality, we knew just enough to get ourselves in financial trouble and fool ourselves about what we really knew.

After careful consideration we decided to order 10,000 T-shirts, 5,000 tote bags, and 10,000 key chains. To get the product would cost close to $34,000 dollars, but considering the volume we'd move we felt like that was a drop in the bucket. We calculated that we would make about $160,000 gross from the conference. Even after the ministry took it's cut, we'd still have close to $100,000 left, which would make the deal more than worthwhile.

We only had about $5,000 that we could put into the project, so we began to ask every person who we thought had money to contribute to the project. I approached one of the deacons, Julius Koonce, about investing in the project. He owned a company that built custom computers and was financially stable. We offered him a 25% return on his investment, a handsome return. After taking a day to think it over and talk with his wife, he called me the next day, told me he believed in what we were doing, and stroked a $10,000 check.

Time was running out and so were our options. I decided to contact John, my friend from church who made the custom suits for the Bishop. Since our conversation at UPS we had developed something of a relationship. I told him about our experience with Deacon Koonce, but that we were still short about $20,000. John began to minister to me about God's word and His ways, saying that many times, God will give us all we need for all that we want. Though we only had $15,000 and needed $34,000, it was possible for God to favor us to the point where we could get everything that we needed. He then told us that the Holy Spirit instructed him to tell us we had all we need for all we want, and that we needed to simply **trust GOD!!!**

Although, I appreciated the gesture, I looked at it more like he didn't want to give us any money and had used prophecy as a cop-out to telling us no. While he talked, I kind of blocked out what he was

God, I ain't trying to hear all that!

saying because it wasn't what I wanted to hear. I just acted like he was giving me a good word, but it went in one ear and out the other.

Get Ready! Get Ready! Get Ready . . . for Disaster!

In the midst of our business struggles, my best friend Judas got married to a girl named Denise from Minneapolis. At the wedding I met a lot of Denise's friends. I was particularly drawn to one of her friends named Chandra. She was a corporate attorney that lived in Minneapolis, but was originally from Georgia. She had a magnetic personality and because she was from Atlanta we had an immediate connection. We talked on occasion after the wedding and our conversation was always interesting because she was so business oriented.

When I felt like my options were running out, I decided to present the Bishop Man opportunity to her. While she immediately saw the potential of the deal, she was a bit concerned that there was no contractual agreement, considering the fact that there was so much money involved. Being a corporate lawyer, she insisted that a contract be in place before she would consider putting up any money. With that said, I completed a contract outlining the details and splits and had Sam sign it. Once he'd signed it, I showed it to Chandra, and she agreed to invest $22,000 at 20% interest. We had the money we needed and I was nervous knowing the entire business was riding on this one conference. We had to hit either a home run or we were sure to strike out.

By the time we purchased everything and prepared for our trip, we had no money left except to cover our hotel expenses. Had we not had a couple of people to allow us to borrow money, we wouldn't have even been able to eat. The conference was scheduled for the Superdome and, considering the huge following of the Bishop Man ministry, we expected more than half of the over 50,000 seats to be full. Looking back, there were a lot of signs that alluded to what we should have expected. The problem was, we chose to ignore them.

People in the lobby from the ministry would stare at us and not say a word. Then there was the merchandise. None of it arrived on time, which caused great concern. Sam had made it clear that he didn't trust us. He insisted that we do nothing in the way of selling products. To make it worse, the people that he had selling were not all from his ministry; some were volunteers from local churches. How could he trust them any more than he could trust us? On top of that, Sam brought his brother John to oversee the project and handle the money. Thursday morning, we met John at the Superdome to count all of the merchandise. He took an authoritative role, which caused us to bump heads right from the start. He approached me the night before the conference started, looking a bit irritated. He asked me why the Bishop Man's name wasn't on the shirts. Angry at his imposition I was going to ignore him, but decided to answer his questions. I told him the reason we decided not to put the Bishop's name on the shirts was so that we could sell them after the conference was over if there were any left. I told John that I thought that the conference was focused on the lives of women being changed, not whether or not Bishop's name was on the shirt. The conference wasn't about the Bishop Man, he was just a vessel. John became furious, saying that I didn't have the ministry's interest at heart when I printed the shirts. He walked away saying that I had a lot to learn.

Right before we were about to sit down for the service, Sam came to us and said that he needed our help selling the merchandise because they didn't have enough volunteers. We took the opportunity because we were still trying to make a good impression, in spite of all of that had happened. Sam set us up at the two tables. Palmer and I would be working with John. The volunteers would work primarily with the tape and book tables.

I noticed very quickly that the number in attendance that Thursday wasn't close to the 30,000 - 35,000 that Sam had predicted. I brushed it off as it being a result of the first day of the conference being on a Thursday. Then I learned that there was one important fact that Sam hadn't told us. This was the first year that they had charged a registration fee for the conference. That was something that should've been asked and discovered while planning. I was kicking myself the rest of the trip. We had failed to prepare properly.

The service that night was powerful and it seemed like every woman in attendance was impacted. The problem was that the numbers were low. There appeared to be less than 10,000. Adding to my worries was the fact that after the service, the women weren't buying anything. There were some sales, but not nearly the number I had expected. Because of the poor attendance, we had to up the price of the shirts from $15 to $20, which surely impacted sales. Sam reluctantly agreed to up the price, but seemed nonchalant when I addressed my attendance concern. He even told me that he didn't care whether or not we made any money, as long as the ministry did. That burned me up, especially considering that he was the Bishop Man's right hand man.

I tried to make the best out of a bad situation. At least I understood why John acted the way he did. If his brother cared nothing about our business, he wasn't going to either. Regardless, my pride and anger were rising steadily and I couldn't help but think that the Bishop Man knew exactly what his men were doing and did nothing about it.

Though sales increased as the conference continued, I came to the realization that the big payday that we thought we were going to have wasn't going to happen. I heard from various volunteers that the attendance numbers were low; there were still under 15,000 women as of Friday night. By the last day, we had sold a lot of items in relation to the number of people that were there, but we had bought far more than we needed. The words of John Gatling kept running through my head. He'd told me that God had given us exactly what we needed, but I didn't listen and went and borrowed more money than I needed. Had I just used the money that we'd had when we talked to John, we'd have sold out. That's when I realized an important lesson: ***God will take what you have to create what you need.*** Because He knows your situation, He will either provide for what you are asking, or provide based on what He knows your need will be. Though He gave me the solution, I wasn't listening and it cost us.

On the last day of the conference, I approached Sam about selling at the upcoming Manpower conference to be held in Greensboro. He told us that he would think about it. When I contended that we lost money on this deal, he reiterated that it was our problem, not his and that our sales were not a determining factor in his decision. At this point, my anger turned to sadness. I found myself begging this man. All my pride was slipping away. I realized my mistake was assuming that doing business with Christians would be different.

We worked hard to make a quality product, even after not being trusted. We still had to see the deal through and come up with the money we'd promised, which in a word, devastated me. As we walked back to our hotel room, tears formed in my eyes and all I could ask God was "Why?"

A Message to God

God can and will speak to us in many different ways, but we must be listening. I just wanted to know why this had to happen to us. A good friend of mine named Marilyn had came to the conference with us. I liked Marilyn because she was no nonsense and loved the Lord. She would tell you like it was, even if you didn't want to hear it. Because of her relationship with God and her heart for worship, I expected God to have already consulted her about the situation. When I asked her how this could happen, all she said was, "I don't know." When I looked at my partners, Phil, Page, and Doom, I didn't need them to say anything. Their eyes spoke volumes.

When we got to the room, I cried myself to sleep. I hated the fact that my own selfish desires had caused me to miss out on what God had been ready to provide. I didn't feel like praying; I didn't think I had it in me. The next morning, we were getting ready to go to breakfast before heading home when Marilyn asked if she could talk with me. She told me that she knew I was hurting and she hurt for me. God had given her something. My ears perked with anticipation. I was desperate and needed something. She pulled out five pages of notes that she said the Lord gave her last night. She said that God woke her up at 3:00 a.m. and proceeded to give her the following:

> *Dear Ken -*
> *Only those who go through can lead the way for others. You're not being punished; you've done your best. Your heart is right. Lift up your head and take courage. Go forth with boldness knowing that I am with you. Confidence is the key, confidence in me*

first. Seek me first, seek me diligently, seek my righteousness. You are called to righteousness. I called you out of your mother's womb for such a day as this. Do not waiver at the things you have learned. Consider David and Paul. Lift up your head. I'm doing something in your life and you're being remade. The world has failed you but I never will. When things of old have been put away, when you stand before me completely naked, an open and available vessel, then, then, then will you hear from heaven. I will heal your land. I will prosper you. I am not a man that I should lie. Waiver not in my promises; I am with you always.

Those words stayed with me for some time, and I came to realize that God will give you all that you need and want. It is greed that will cause you to ignore the obvious signs and lead you to failure only to have to learn a lesson the hard way. We were so involved in how much money we were going to make we neglected to look at the situation rationally. We went into it blindly. When all was said and done we were left with tons of unsold inventory and a debt of $35,000. Not only was it the debt that weighed on me, we owed this money to friends and members of the church.

My greed caused me to get in this situation, and hindered my success. I realized that God was using this situation to remold me and change me to become a better person. Man's motivation in life

117

God, I ain't trying to hear all that!

should be how he can give, and not how he can
take.

God, I ain't trying to hear all that!

God, I ain't trying to hear all that!

CHAPTER EIGHT

The Bottom Falls Out

I never thought in my wildest dreams that I would have hit rock bottom just after being featured on CNN, BET, and QVC. The bottom just fell out. We were broke, busted, and disgusted. I knew the first thing I had to do was come to grips with my emotions and face reality. We had borrowed money from close friends, friends of friends, extended ourselves with suppliers; it seemed like we owed everyone money.

In the aftermath of the situation with the Bishop Man, I began to do something that I should've been doing long before; I began to pray consistently, keeping a prayer journal. Revelation began to come in so many different forms that I had to write it down just to remember it.

The following is one of my journal entries:
Finally, I am doing something that I should've been doing long ago. In prayer

this morning, I got the revelation to do what I've been putting off doing for years. I think my reason for doing it is because it will help someone in the future. I think my testimony will inspire and encourage many people. I'm at the lowest point of my life financially, but at my highest point ever in my relationship with God, and I believe that's what's going to get us through this situation. I'm reminded of the word from God that Marilyn gave me at the women's conference in New Orleans. This week's events have been extremely humbling. First the Bishop Man's Ministries deceived me. We were depending on them to order some product. This was Sam's way of helping us out. I had a problem with their unwillingness to admit any responsibility for our surplus in the first place. Had they not told me there would be 35,000 women at the conference, I would never have ordered that much product. I do feel responsible. I should've drawn up a contract with the ministry for the first conference stating that if we gave the ministry 55% of the proceeds we would be able to go to the next conference regardless of other outside circumstances. I learned so much about man through this incident. It doesn't matter whether you are a man of God or not, business is business. I realize now that God is my only source of direction.

Sam had sent a check for our portion of the $110,000 in sales. It equated to a little over $50,000 dollars. The problem was that this wasn't enough to pay everyone that we owed, including my friend, Chandra Houston. She had believed in us and our plan and we'd let her down. We had never completely paid her from the women's conference, and now we had a bill from the men's conference on top of that. In total, we were in the hole for around $100,000 from this deal.

We had a meeting to decide who we would pay with the money and how much they were going to get paid. We owed FedEx $5,000 for shipping, Chandra Houston around $35,000, and Unitex $45,000. Add another $15,000 or so for miscellaneous expenses, and you're right at $100,000. Chandra was a successful corporate lawyer that I had developed a good relationship with over the years. We had always admired each other because of our motivation. She took a chance on us twice and we failed to deliver both times. How was I going to tell her that we couldn't give her all of her money, or for that matter, anything close to what we owed her? I had to muster up the strength to tell her the truth about what had happened. She responded the way I thought she would. She told me that she felt like she had been lied to and betrayed because I didn't tell her the entire situation from the beginning, leading her to believe that things were better for us than they were. She was right. I realized I had misled her. I admitted to that. It was never my motive to deceive her, but I was more concerned with getting the money than in my integrity, and I didn't want to reveal any information that would jeopardize this. The thing that pierced my heart was when I heard the despair and disappointment in her voice from being out thousands of dollars. It was at that point that I realized, I was her Sam; I was no better than he was. I'd criticized Sam's character and saw him as a cheat, never taking a moment to look at myself and see how I used others for my own personal gain.

When the walls came crumbling down I eventually had to look at myself and I didn't like what I saw. I felt horrible and didn't know what to do or where to turn. Finally, after agonizing over this, I went to my father for help. I discussed with him how we were trying to work out a payment program with some of our creditors and keep our cash flow going. My father suggested we approach the Martin Luther King, Jr. Center in Atlanta about carrying some of our commemorative watches. I was excited about the idea since I had so much admiration and respect for Dr. King. The Summer Olympics were scheduled to be in Atlanta that year, which meant that there would be considerable tourist traffic at all of the landmarks. We liked the idea but I was hesitant to try and strike up another deal. My father could sense my apprehension and suggested he would make the contact and try to arrange the deal. It made good sense. He had sold watches to individuals and companies for us in the past and knew the product. I had no doubt that he could represent us thoroughly and get a deal through.

God, I ain't trying to hear all that!

Dad set a meeting with Susan Stainrod, the gift shop manager in the King Center, and they immediately hit it off. She saw the profit potential because of the upcoming Olympics. At this point my dad got me involved in the process, giving me Susan's number so that I could try to convince her boss that the watches would sell.

My dad was proud of my accomplishments even though I felt like I had failed. He made it a point to let this woman know that the company I'd started had come to national prominence, and how proud he was of my present accomplishments. He told her about the newspaper and magazine articles, the success with selling our products on television, and even our connections with the Bishop Man's Ministries. The only thing I was concerned with was of people getting an impression that things were better than they were. After the incident with Chandra, I wanted to be straightforward with everyone.

When I called Susan I found that my dad had done all of the selling that needed to be done to convince her. All she had to do was sell her manager, Johnny Mack on the idea. The impression that I got from Susan was that Johnny Mack was a cool guy, but all about the bottom line. If he didn't see the profit potential, he wouldn't make the investment, regardless of how much he liked the product. He was extremely hard on product that was new and relatively unproved, and that was the category our watches fell into.

When Susan called me back about a week later she said that Johnny had seen the product and liked it, but it was like pulling teeth. The initial deal was for 100 watches as a test run. If things went well, they would order a lot more for the Olympics. All she needed was a purchase order and we could get the ball rolling. I faxed the purchase order to her the same day, and within a week my dad received the check for $2,900! I was shocked because this was the first company we'd worked with that paid us that quickly. When Dad called me to inform me that he had the check, he added that Susan had told him that she had to "go through a lot to get this deal to go through." This stuck with me, because those were sentiments that she had expressed when we talked. Why did she find it necessary to reiterate them to my father? I let it go for the time being because we had the cash in hand and wanted to get the watches out to them. We believed that when they started selling, Johnny would re-order very quickly, or at least that was our plan.

The watches sold well out of the gate. I made it a point to stay in constant contact with Susan, and we began to develop a good relationship. I liked her because she was cordial and energetic, and liked to get things done. I called one day, and when she answered I could hear the despair in her voice. It took some coaxing but I finally got her to open up about what was wrong. She told me that she was tired of working at the King Center because they were so corrupt in their business dealings. This shocked and disturbed me, especially with us doing business with them. This validated her continued frustration in all that she had to go through to get the deal done for us. I asked her what she meant by

corrupt because I wanted to know what to look out
for. Frustrated, she replied that they used her to do
their "dirty work". The more I listened, the more it
sounded like the King Center was run by a mob and
she was a hit person. She told me that they had done
many business deals wrong, which elevated my
level of concern with our deal. She said that the
reason we were paid so quickly was because she
personally got our money.

"The King Center has a negative track
record when it comes to paying vendors," she told
me. "They've lied to vendors, saying they were
going to pay with no intention of paying. I've been
told to lie. The powers that be never intend to pay
them their money, and I'm always stuck in the
middle."

She named vendor after vendor that the
King Center had swindled out of a lot of money,
and who would probably never get paid. Though I
was listening, the impact of what she was saying
didn't really weigh on me, even though we were
doing business with them. After all, we had our
money and as far as I was concerned, that was their
problem. I felt like Susan was in our corner and
could watch our back if things got ugly. I was
impressed with her honesty.

A few weeks later my dad called me and
told me he had just gotten off the phone with Susan.
The King Center had agreed to do 2,000 watches for
the upcoming Summer Olympics, which was only
eight weeks away. I couldn't believe it! He said that
Susan was going to fax over a signed purchase
order so we could proceed with ordering the

watches. I stressed to him that I could not proceed without the purchase order and that if I didn't receive it in a day, I would call Susan. After we hung up, I was still in shock. This was an order worth over $59,000, and it was only their second order with us. Just like clockwork, the purchase order fax came through. I proceeded to call my banker, Mike Wilkerson and get money from our line of credit. It was no problem getting it approved because it was the King Center and they had ordered from us in the past. I sent $20,000 to our overseas manufacturer to have the watches made and all systems were go, even putting a rush on the order to be sure we stayed within our time constraints. Things were going well and everyone felt good about the progress of the deal. I felt like I was given a second chance and if all went well, I would be able pay back the people who had placed their trust in me and had given us cash for the conferences. I'd learned about character and realized I had a chance to fix what I had done wrong. This was the break we needed to get things back on track.

One day, out of the clear blue sky, I get an unexpected call from Susan. I could tell from her voice that something was not right. Struggling to get her words out she said, "Johnny Mack's reneged on the deal."

"What!" I replied. "He can't do that! I've already spent $20,000 getting the watches made!"

I began to unravel inside, thinking of the $20,000 loan that we had gotten to get the deal going. At this point, all of the things Susan had said in our earlier conversation began to make sense. In that moment, I became one of the "other vendors." When Johnny Mack reneged I saw the type of operation that they were running. The first thing I wanted to do was hear it from the horse's mouth himself, because I couldn't believe a place like the King Center would do business so terribly.

"I don't know if you're going to get the truth out of him, but you can try," she warned. "Before you talk to him, I'll tell you what I know. From my understanding, they were trying to get a line of credit, somewhere in the neighborhood of one million; however, they were turned down for the money. Honestly, I don't think they stuck it to you guys on purpose, it was just poor management and they truly don't have the money to go through with the deal."

I didn't care why the deal wasn't going through. We were still stuck with the $20,000 loss. To my surprise, Susan put Johnny Mack on the phone so I could talk to him. I started off calm. I didn't see the point in having a hostile conversation. I told him I was aware that they had canceled the orders, and he said it was true. When I asked him why, he responded that they'd just decided not to order the watches. This made me extremely upset, but I refused to show it at that point. I reminded him that we had a signed purchase order and informed him that we had spent the money to get the watches produced because they needed the watches in time for the Olympics. In a nonchalant manner he told me that we had two choices, either forget about the order, or send us the watches on consignment and at the end of the Olympics they would pay us on whatever they sold. He reiterated that those were my only two choices.

I was steaming mad inside but remained calm. After talking with my business partners, we felt we had no other option but to agree to give them the watches on consignment. We needed to recover our material cost and wanted to keep good faith with our vendors. When I told my banker, Mike Wilkerson, about what happened, he was pissed at everybody. He was pissed at them because he thought they were a business thriving on integrity. He was pissed at us because he felt we should've examined all possible avenues. I felt bad because Mike, like those before him, had taken a chance on us and we didn't deliver. Our vendor in Hong Kong got the watches to us in a timely manner as always, and we sent the watches on to the King Center. It took us forever to pack those watches and while packing them, all we could think about was whether or not things would work out. I was on edge during the entire Olympics, wondering if we'd sold any watches. I would call Susan and ask her how sales were going. She would tell me that she didn't have an accurate count, but warned me that many of the vendors in the area, as well as the King Center, were complaining that traffic was being directed away from the historically black sections. She said all the vendors in the neighborhood were suffering from this, that there was television coverage of black vendors and even threats of lawsuits against the city. People were saying that they had used their life savings and taken mortgages on their homes to purchase products to sell at the Olympics.

This wasn't comforting news to us, particularly after being railroaded in the deal. Again, Susan shot us straight and I appreciated that even though it wasn't what I wanted to hear. By this time the Olympics were coming to an end. I got in contact with Susan again. I could tell by the tone of her voice that she didn't want to tell me something. I asked her how the sales were on the watches, knowing that because of the traffic situation the numbers had probably suffered some.

"Ken, to be honest with you, we've sold less than twenty watches."

At that moment, I became sick. "Twenty watches!" I thought to myself. "I can sell twenty watches in the street!"

"It's because of the traffic. We haven't had much in sales for the entire event," she said, trying to comfort me.

Though she kept talking, I heard nothing she said after that. Twenty watches was all that rang in my head. My heart was in my stomach. We'd hit rock bottom before, but now the floor had fallen out. When a man is down and reaches his lowest point, it is there that the true character of the person is exposed. I was torn open and lost. How could this be happening to me? Why? I realized God was teaching me about character and leaving an imprint.

A few weeks later I get an unexpected call from Susan; she sounded upbeat and excited.

"I have some good news for you," she said.

"I sure could use some," I responded.

"While tallying up sales to figure out what we owed vendors, some of your watches came up missing. Some people thought they were in the hallway, others thought they were in storage, but no one could find them," she said.

I cut her off. "That means you owe me for the watches you can't find because they can't be returned to me!"

"That's exactly what it means!" Susan replied, just as excited as I was.

I shouted, "Thank You, Jesus!" at the top of my lungs.

It was a miracle. The lost watches totaled $18,000, all of which they had to pay to us. Though we were still in the hole, it was a much smaller hole, and we felt like we had a glimmer of hope.

One thing that still bothered me was something Susan had turned us on to from the beginning. With the King Center, money owed did not equal money paid. Weeks went by and we still didn't collect all of our money, or most of it for that matter. Weeks eventually turned to months and our frustration mounted. As time passed we came to the realization that we weren't going to get paid. We decided to contact a collection agency and have them work on it. About two weeks after contacting the agency I got a phone call from the Trans-world office in Atlanta. The man who had been working on our case informed me that he was sure he would be able to get some of our money back. A few days passed and he called me again, saying that he'd talked to Johnny Mack about the situation. He said that Johnny Mack was very cordial and was willing to make amends and keep it out of court. I was shocked because I knew we had signed a letter agreeing to consignment. When I asked him about how the letter played into the equation, he told me that Johnny Mack was resistant at first because of it, but when they requested a copy of the letter so that they could review it, he'd been unable to find it. Apparently it had disappeared.

When it was all over, Trans-world and the King Center agreed on a settlement of an additional $15,000, of which Trans-world got half. Though it was a far cry from $41,000, it was something. I learned that many times, what we perceive to be the solution to our problems can end up being the cause of greater problems. Though this could be looked at as a negative situation, I knew that all things happen for a reason. Every situation tests and challenges one's character, forever changing it. I learned a lot from Susan about integrity and honesty. She never sugarcoated the situation like I did with Chandra, persuading her to feel everything was going great when it really wasn't. Integrity is about being honest, sincere and putting the feelings of others first.

After all of this I was left with the one person I knew I could talk to and who would listen: God. I began to pray and analyze my current situation to figure out how I got here. I was forced to look deep inside and really analyze who I was and what I could change in my character to keep this type of event from happening ever again. I finally came to the realization that what we go through in life is necessary to the development of our character. Character literally means to make an imprint. That's why it hurts so bad when God is developing character in you; he's using an episode or experience to make an imprint on you.

If success is knowing God, than I am committed to building a personal relationship with God through his son, Jesus Christ. No person will ever reach their God-given potential apart from Him. These personal relationships include prayer. Prayer has been the one thing that has pulled me through the tough times. Many nights I've lain in bed praying, but I was never defeated. I understood that this journey was an adventure that provided experiences and that these have built my character and shaped my destiny.

Knowing your purpose in life is the second ingredient to success. My adversity has helped me know my purpose in life. God has allowed me to take this course in my life so that I could understand the real meaning of life. Despite my earlier aspirations of money and power, my true dream is to help others fulfill their dreams. My adversity forced me to look inside and the real me beyond material things. I realized that who I was inside was more important than what I owned or my occupation. Adversity was necessary to the changes in my character. Now I take what I have learned, and use those experiences to help others. If one person can learn from my mistakes, if one individual can take what I've been through and use it to find their way in life, I have fulfilled my purpose.

Growing to my Maximum Potential and being a successful businessman has always been my desire. All of the adversity during those failed business deals gave me tools that I needed to become a successful businessman. What I didn't know at the time was that everything I learned would serve me well in subsequent business deals. I learned to conduct business with integrity and the foresight to see problems before they arise. I paid for this education, and it has served me well. The area that I'm growing in the most is to seek God before I enter into any business deals. Seeking God along with paying my tithes consistently. My business is well on its way to making the millions I envisioned from the beginning.

Sowing Seeds to Help Others

Some people tell themselves that as soon as they achieve considerable success or discover some unseen talent, they will turn their attention to making a difference in the lives of others. I was one of those people. I continually forced all my energy on myself. I finally realized that many of my failures came because I dedicated most of my time to looking out for number one. I developed a new way of thinking, where others come first.

My new motto is "Give that which you want." My focus is on giving others the things I want in my life. I want love, so I give it. I want compassion, so I give it. I want understanding, so I give it. I want knowledge, so I give it. I want money, so I give it. These are just a few of the things that I sow into the lives of others. The principal of giving to benefit others has given me more than I ever could have imagined. To succeed personally you must try to help others. I've heard Zig Ziglar say, "You can get everything you want if you help enough other people get what they want."

Live Your Dreams

It doesn't matter whether your objectives are in the area of business, sports, school ministry, finance or relationships. The only way you can get ahead is to face adversity and learn from it. Every dream was realized because of dedication to this process. Adversity lies at the heart of every success. The process of achievement comes through repeated failures, adversity and the constant struggle to climb to higher level.

Concede that you must make it through some adversity in order to succeed. Acknowledge that you have to experience the occasional setback to make progress. To achieve your dreams, we all must embrace adversity and make failure a regular part of your life.

CHAPTER NINE:

The Sweet is Never As Sweet Without the Sour

I have often asked the question why? Why did it happen this way? Why did it happen to me? GOD, why does it seem like the people who care nothing about you seem to have so much success? Why is it that the ones who love you seem to have so many problems? Each time things didn't go the way I planned, I blasted GOD and myself with questions I knew I would probably never receive satisfactory answers for.

Looking back, I am able to reflect on all my adversity and say with all honesty that if I had to do it over again, I wouldn't change a thing. All of the adversity and failures are the things that have made me a success. My definition of success is beyond money. I can truly say that I am succeeding at life.

136

God, I ain't trying to hear all that!

Remember, success is:

1. Knowing God
2. Knowing your purpose in life
3. Growing to reach your maximum potential
4. Sowing seeds to help others.

I have come to realize that success is not a destination; not a place where you arrive one day. Instead, it is the journey you take. Your success comes from what you do every day. It is a process.

Resolution

I finally came to the realization that adversity and failures were there because that was the way that GOD designed it. There is no coincidence. Whether we believe it or not, GOD is using our current situation or circumstance to help us fulfill our destiny. He wants us to be successful in life, and He uses our adversity to become successful people. God uses our adversity for two reasons. The first reason is to let us know how much we need Him. Though He wants us to be successful, He doesn't want us to be a success apart from him. The second reason is, He uses our adversity to build our character. Once we become the success that He wills for all of our lives, He wants us to have a character that is like Him.

I asked for Strength.............
And God gave me Difficulties to make me strong.

God, I ain't trying to hear all that!

I asked for Wisdom………..
And God gave me Problems to solve

I asked for Prosperity…….
And God gave me a Brain and Brawn to work

I asked for Courage……..
And God gave me Danger to overcome

I asked for Love…..
And God gave me Troubled people to help

I asked for Favor
And God gave me Opportunities.

I received nothing I wanted…….
I received everything I needed!

The Butterfly

One day, a man was walking in his yard when he chanced upon a small object. He bent and picked it up. It was a cocoon. Inside, he knew, was a butterfly waiting to emerge. He put it in the crook of his old Oak tree. One day a small opening appeared. He sat and watched the butterfly for several hours as it struggled to force its body through that little hole. Then it seemed to stop making any progress. It appeared as if it had gotten as far as it could, and it could go no further.

So the man decided to help the butterfly. He took a pair of scissors and snipped off the remaining bit of the cocoon. The butterfly emerged easily, but its body was swollen and it's wings small and shriveled. The man continued to watch the butterfly. He somehow expected that, at any moment, the wings would enlarge and expand to be able to support the body, which would contract in time.

Neither happened! In fact, the butterfly spent the rest of its life crawling around with a swollen body and shriveled wings. It was never able to fly. What the man in his kindness and haste did not understand, was that the restricting cocoon and the struggle required for the butterfly to get through the tiny opening was God's way of forcing fluid from the body of the butterfly into its wings so that it would be ready for flight once it achieved its freedom from the cocoon.

Sometimes struggles are exactly what we need in our lives. If God allowed us to go through our lives without any obstacles, it would cripple us. We would not be as strong as we could have been.

We could never fly!

God, I ain't trying to hear all that!

Quick Order Form

Fax Orders: (336) 273 – 4110

Telephone Orders: Call (336) 273 – 1449

E-mail: kcanion@aol.com

Postal Orders: Prosperity Marketing
              510 Franklin Blvd.
              Greensboro, NC 27401

Please send more FREE information on:
❑ Books / Video's   ❑ Seminars / Speaking

Name: _____

Address: _____

City: _____ State: _____ Zip: _____

Telephone: _____

e-mail address: _____

Shipping: $3.00 for first book $2.00 for each additional

Payment: ❑ Check   ❑ Credit Card

                  ❑ VISA   ❑ Mastercard

Card Number: _____

Name on Card: _____

Expiration Date: _____ / _____